TABLE TENNIS

The Skills of the Game

TABLE TENNIS
The Skills of the Game

GORDON STEGGALL
with Peter Hirst

THE CROWOOD PRESS

First published in 1986 by
THE CROWOOD PRESS
Ramsbury, Marlborough
Wiltshire SN8 2HE

British Library Cataloguing in Publication Data

Steggall, Gordon
  Table tennis: the skills of the game.
  1. Table tennis
  I. Title   II. Hirst, Peter
  796.34'6   GV1005

  ISBN 0-946284-67-9

Acknowledgements

Fig 105 by Stephen Line, all other photographs by Ian Ball

Cover photographs by Ian Ball

Line illustrations by Vanetta Joffe

The author thanks Alan Cooke and Fiona Elliott for their help
with the demonstration photographs; and the ETTA, the ESTTA
and Dunlop Sports Co. Ltd for permission to reproduce the
Dunlop Skills Award Scheme.

Series Adviser David Bunker, Lecturer, Loughborough University
of Technology

Typeset by Alacrity Phototypesetters, Banwell Castle, Weston-super-Mare
Printed in Great Britain

Contents

Gordon Steggall has been Chairman of the National Coaching Committee of the English Table Tennis Association since 1967. Still an active player, he played the tournament circuit for many years before concentrating on teaching. He is a Three Star Diploma Coach specialising in the training of coaches, and is also the National Organiser of the Dunlop Skills Award Scheme.

Peter Hirst is Director of Coaching for the New Zealand Table Tennis Association. His previous post was that of National Coach for the English Table Tennis Association, in which capacity he captained many England teams. His practical experience of many years of coaching at all levels has been invaluable to officials and coaches alike.

Gordon Steggall's approach to table tennis is straightforward, down to earth and uncomplicated. His simple instructions can produce that little extra that grass roots players are looking for, and the more advanced players can also benefit if they consider the text very carefully and relate it to their own game. All players realise they have plenty of room for improvement and this book could very well open the way.

Compiled by a person whose background in coaching in England is unsurpassed and whose knowledge of the subject is well known and respected, this book is recommended for players and coaches alike.

Tom Blunn
Chairman, ETTA

I owe a great deal to Peter Hirst for my level of play and in particular to the fundamental principles outlined in this very informative book.

Alan Cooke
England No. 3

Gordon Steggall has had tremendous experience in the coaching and training of players and coaches. This book teaches us all to examine our game more logically and to concentrate on the whole skill rather than isolated stroke production.

Donald Parker
ETTA National Trainer

Gordon Steggall, jointly with the late Jack Carrington, has been the greatest influence on the ETTA Coaching Scheme for the last twenty years. His personality and drive have been the force behind many of the coaches now working throughout England.

Peter Hirst was one of the most respected technical National Coaches in England before becoming Director of Coaching in New Zealand. His ability to communicate table tennis techniques to both coaches and players has been used to advantage in this book.

Peter Charters
Vice Chairman of ETTA
Chairman of the England Selectors

Introduction

Table tennis has been played in various forms since the turn of the century. It was originally known as 'Gossamer' and was played with bats made of dried animal skin stretched over a wooden frame. From this it progressed to 'Ping Pong' and was so popular that world championships were held as far back as 1902.

Most people have attempted to play table tennis at some time in their life. Many holiday camps, hotels and liners have table tennis facilities. It is a game which is available to all kinds of people, young and old, extrovert, athletic and even disabled. There is, however, a great deal of difference between the sport played as a pastime for fun and the more serious side, that of the competitive match player. Those people who are prepared to learn good fundamental principles, often increase their pleasure level to such an extent that many adopt table tennis as a main sporting driving force throughout their life.

The game of table tennis enjoys a large following throughout the world, with over seventy-five countries competing in the biennial world championships. There are over twenty million active registered players throughout the world apart from the many that just play for pleasure and recreation. These numbers may further increase when table tennis becomes an Olympic sport in 1988. There are only a few players who can reach the top of their sport, but there are few sports which offer so many opportunities at every level as table tennis.

As the sport is organised on a world-wide basis, the rules are laid down by the International Table Tennis Federation and administered by national Table Tennis Associations for all official games played within their jurisdiction. Anyone wishing to participate in such a happy and organised game needs to join a registered table tennis club sooner rather than later. The advantages immediately become obvious, with good playing conditions, qualified coaches and better partners with whom to improve.

There is no set rule about the minimum age for taking up table tennis, but very few children under seven years old have the necessary height or co-ordination to be taught a game that will withstand their growing adolescence. Small players could be shown the basics on tables which have had their legs cut down or by standing on gym mats to reduce the table height. At the other end of the scale, there are some extremely respected players in their sixties who did not take up the sport until well into middle age. People with physical handicaps often find ways of compensating for their disability, allowing them to play in one of the thousands of League matches that take place throughout the season.

This book is written for players, both men and women, of all ages, and coaches who wish to raise their standards to increase their chances of success. There is something for everyone, particularly for the eager person willing to build on present abilities using both logical and emotional concepts. The book also aims to encourage all players to review their game and, by using simple analytical processes, increase their ability to compete with even more enjoyment.

1 The Basic Framework

THE SYSTEM

Table tennis could be described as a game of chess played at 100 m.p.h. To play at a high level one needs to have:

1. A strong mental approach.
2. Good technical and tactical ability.
3. A high level of physical fitness.
4. The ability to read a situation.

Table tennis can be all things to all men. It can be:

1. Recreational to the youth club player.
2. Educational to school children.
3. A social event.
4. Therapeutic as gentle exercise to someone who is recovering from illness.
5. A highly skilful physical sport that demands both great speed and stamina.

At the early stages we have to consider what is our overall aim in order to decide how we move forward on the long pleasurable road to achieving our full potential.

True Skill

What is the true skill of table tennis? A common belief is that it is just a collection of strokes. Many coaches make the mistake of only providing for control over strokes in isolated situations, which ultimately leaves enormous gaps in a player's game. This book is written on the basis that true skill is a series of rallies adding up to a game. A rally can be a number of different strokes in any combination. Therefore the joining of those strokes is equally, if not more, important than the strokes themselves.

I describe a rally in table tennis as consisting of:

1. The mechanical components – the strokes.
2. The nuts and bolts to fasten those components – good positioning and recovery.
3. The tuning of the engine – good anticipation and reaction skills.

The most important of those three in my opinion is without doubt the third: good anticipation and reaction skills.

Let us take an example. If the current World Men's Singles Champion was to hit the ball as hard as he was able, with as much spin as he could, then ninety-nine per cent of table tennis players would be able to return that ball consistently well – providing that it was hit to the same place with the same speed and with the same spin. In other words, it is not just the amount of speed on the ball, the amount of spin, or even a combination of the two that gives the advantage. A good player is one who can work out exactly what an opponent has done early enough with regard to speed, spin and direction and then react quickly enough to what he has seen. The aspiring player and the dedicated coach must work together in harmony towards producing the whole skill.

Whole Skill

The whole skill is a balanced sequence of strokes combined into a rally, to achieve the best possible tactical result against an opponent, whilst being acutely aware of his actions and the results of those actions.

We achieve the whole skill by searching the rally for its basic components (strokes) and breaking those down into component parts (the variables). Look for the advantages of those variables and then compile them into a logical learning sequence.

It is important to be aware of the match situation because what you do from choice is not always what is done from necessity. The purpose of practice is to reproduce choice, gradually introducing additional loads to cope with the necessity.

Variables

Length (Fig 1)

Length is the distance that the bat travels whenever contact is made with the ball. In nearly every situation and at every level this should be kept to a minimum on the basis that the less you do, the less could go wrong. The overall aim is to concentrate on judging the ball and not to worry about swinging the bat. You are then left to judge the result of your actions which are the only true tests of technique instead of becoming over concerned at the length and direction of swing.

To achieve a maximum degree of control it would be wise to attempt fifty per cent of the swing before contact and fifty per cent after.

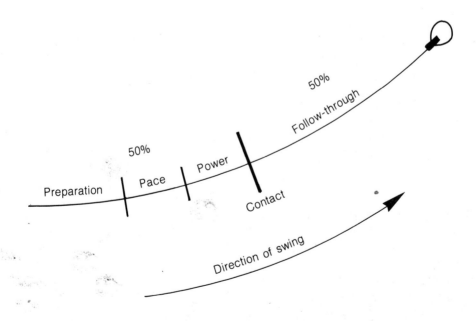

Fig 1   As play becomes more competitive, the follow-through should be reduced to thirty degrees if possible.

The follow-through should decelerate towards a neutral position with the top of the bat pointing to where the ball has travelled. This will allow you to go easily into the next stroke.

It is important to remember that rather than fast jerky actions, you should try to achieve a good rhythm aiming to feel the ball on the bat. This will enhance the level of control.

The tactical advantages of a short stroke is that the opponent has less information to read, and you have more recovery time enabling you to take the ball as early as possible putting the opposition under more pressure.

Timing (Figs 2 & 3)

Timing is the point when the ball is struck during its flight. When possible, it is better to make contact with the ball within the range of the peak bounce. There are several advantages from making contact at this point:

1. Striking the ball at a point above net height increases the angle towards the target area, enabling the ball to travel in a straight line and thus allowing it to travel with maximum speed and power.

2. It allows a much greater range of target area.

3. It is generally accepted that people develop a timing point which remains permanently set throughout their playing career and that it is set within the first six to twelve months of them starting to play table tennis on a regular basis.

In a practice situation the majority of people can do most things, but in a high pressure match situation it is very common for a person to play by instinct thus reverting back to a timing set during the early period of play.

To achieve the greatest effect from hitting the ball at a relatively high point, it is advantageous to use a relatively closed angle of bat (*Fig 3*). This brings the ball to the play-

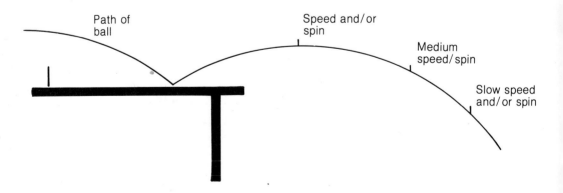

Fig 2   Timing the ball.

ing surface more easily, especially when speed as well as spin is required.

The direction of swing should be close to horizontal. The bat should travel in the same direction as the ball is to travel to offer a greater degree of control. This way there is a more definite contact between bat and ball allowing a better feel.

If you see that your opponent allows the ball to drop to table level or below, you can guarantee that he will be unable to hit with his maximum speed and power. He will have to settle for less speed and perhaps try for a high degree of spin.

Try to always hit the ball at its highest point, thus achieving the maximum range of stroke and target. This will give your opponent the maximum range of options to work out in a very limited space of time.

Table Position (Fig 4)

Table position is the distance that a person plays in relation to the table. This position should be as close as possible with the ball being taken as early as possible. Striking the ball early offers several benefits:

1. Extra time – if your opponent is striking the ball level with his base line (the edge of the

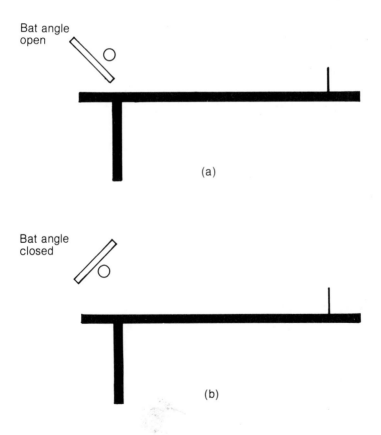

Fig 3   (a) Bat angle open; (b) bat angle closed.

table) and you are hitting it level with yours, then both of you have equal decision-making time (if the ball is travelling at a constant speed). If the speed is too great for you, one answer is to drop back approximately one metre, thus gaining approximately half a second. At first it would appear that you have gained an advantage until you appreciate the fact that it also takes the ball the same length of time to return to the base line where you could have made contact in the first place. This gives your opponent twice as much time, i.e. one second. There

is, therefore, a good argument to suggest that if you are in difficulty, you should try to gain time by adopting a position much nearer to the table to gain the full second for yourself, forcing your opponent back and only allowing him the half second.

2. By being near the table, the angle of target is widened considerably. This allows a greater degree of accuracy *(Fig 4)*.

3. The angle available to your opponent remains the same but the distance is reduced for you. This offers less chance of mistakes:

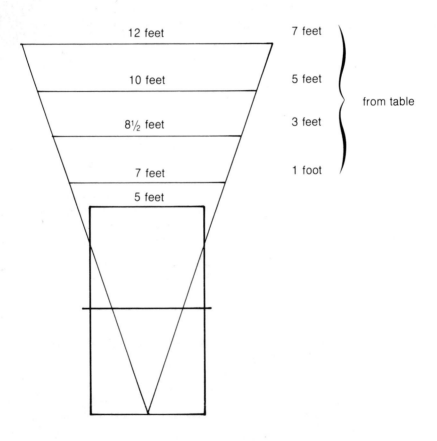

Fig 4   *As you move away from the table, you will have to cover extra area.*

Fig 5   Alan Cooke in the ready position.

Fig 6   Fiona Elliott in the ready position,
which should be adopted at all times.

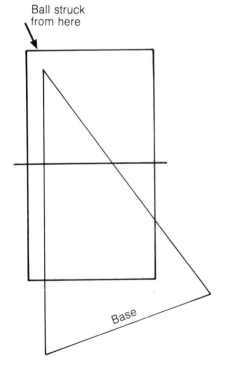

Ball struck
from here

Base

Fig 7   The base moves with the line
of play.

Base (Figs 5 to 7)

Base is the area on which the body rests; in other words, the position of the feet in relation to where the ball is to be struck. The aim is to establish balance between maximum stability of body balance and take-off speed in any direction.

In general, the feet should be placed marginally wider than shoulder width, with the weight placed towards the inside of the balls of your feet. This enables you to move quickly in any direction. You should adopt this attitude at all times between and when executing strokes so as not to be caught off balance.

A tip is to adopt a base position in relation to where the ball has just been struck and not in relation to the table. Remember that the table is in a fixed position. The important factors include the opponent and the ball, so the location of the feet is dictated purely by the position of the ball.

The Basic Framework

Body Action (Figs 8 to 12)

Body action is the movement that is possible once an area of base has been established.
The formula for stability is:

1. The area of base of the body (feet position).
2. The height of the centre of gravity.
3. The horizontal distance from the centre of gravity to the pivoting edge (either foot).

The aim is to achieve a high degree of balance working to the above formula, because the more balanced you are, the more likely you are to maintain a good level of control. This is achieved by maintaining a good base (feet slightly wider than the shoulders).

Adopt a low crouched posture with head slightly forward and the backside out, and the centre of gravity remaining in a position between the feet. It is advisable for you to maintain this through co-ordinated effort

Fig 8   A good stance.

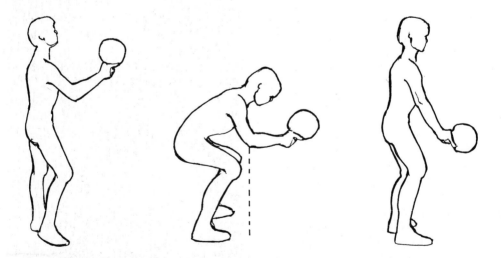

Fig 9   Examples of poor stance.

Fig 10   Preparation.

Fig 11   Contact.

whilst achieving a good overall rhythm. It is this rhythm that will assist you to maintain a high level of control.

You should think in terms of the main power originating from the base, transferring through the legs and body and culminating in an arm action. The body action, by turning the upper part, helps to generate a large proportion of the force. It is also a main contributing factor in deception of direction, by delaying or advancing the timing point slightly whilst maintaining the same movement.

Note: coaches can short-cut the learning process by teaching the rhythm of forehand strokes with the players holding their playing wrists with their free hand. The palm of the free hand should be placed on the lowest part of the playing wrist. This encourages a pivoting effect from the waist which increases the body mass in a forward direction, as well as developing a better overall rhythm.

Fig 12   Follow-through.

The Basic Framework

Free Arm (Figs 13 to 15)

The free arm is the hand and arm not used to hit the ball. The aims of the free arm are threefold:

1. To assist balance when moving.
2. To help with upper body rotation.
3. To assist with orientation of the ball to the upper part of the body.

The free hand is loosely described as pointing to the ball. This provides an additional reference point to the bat, encouraging you to make contact with the ball in the same position in relation to the upper body each time. The internationals make contact with the ball at a naturally comfortable distance and height in relation to the upper body, which can be changed to provide tactical advantage with deception.

    Teaching tip: teach that the free hand should point to the ball.

Fig 14 Note that Alan's free arm is pointing to the ball.

Fig 13 Gradually take your free arm away to the correct position.

Fig 15 Fiona again showing a good position of the free arm.

Bat Arm (Figs 16 to 18)

'Bat arm' is everything that the bat hand and arm does, which includes many of the finer points and subtleties of the sport.

The aim is to achieve as high a range of speed and spin as possible whilst maintaining pressure on your opponent. Judge the results of your actions by the degree of difficulty for the opponent and not the ease of executing the strokes. Think in terms of:

1. Elbow – with a ninety degree angle providing most of the control.
2. Shoulder – producing the more powerful strokes.
3. Wrist – being the fastest moving joint providing speed.

In every sense both speed and power are judged as being the same, but in table tennis terms it is the way that they are produced and in what situation which highlights the difference. Imagine a ball which has been lifted high and has very little forward speed; it would require a shoulder action and considerable body action (body mass) to get the ball to travel forwards. Whereas if the approaching ball has considerable forward speed then a shorter, sharper wrist action would provide a similar result.

In general terms, it is advantageous to have the point of contact on the bat at the same level as the playing elbow. This, linked with a low posture, will contribute enormously towards achieving a high level of control. In a normal open rally situation it is difficult to determine beforehand the type and nature of stroke to be played and in which order.

To facilitate the connecting of the various strokes, all strokes should start and finish in the same position; that is with the top edge of the bat pointing in the direction that the ball has travelled. This places the bat midway between backhand and forehand.

Recovery (Fig 19)

Recovery is the position to which you must move between each stroke to provide yourself with a realistic opportunity of controlling the angles of the table available to your opponent. This is dictated by the target chosen which in turn limits the target area available to your opponent.

The aim is to limit the target area of your opponent with accuracy and careful attention to the type of ball you present to him. Simple geometry determines, within limits, the direction of the possible returns. On playing the ball to your opponent's side of the table, you should immediately recover to a near central position along a new imaginary base line, made up from the maximum angles available to your opponent for the

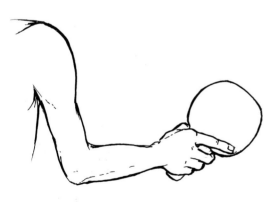

Fig 16   Although normally at 90 degrees, the angle of the elbow moves out and up to 120 degrees for the most powerful kill shots.

Fig 17 The point of contact with the bat is at the same level as the elbow.

Fig 18 The top edge of the bat points in the same direction as the ball is travelling.

return. This means that recovery should be to the 'line of play', rather than adopting a square position in relation to the base line of the table.

Use a stepping action with the nearest foot to the ball moving towards where you wish to meet it. Keep the feet at shoulder width or wider, if possible, whilst maintaining a low centre of gravity.

Tactically, recovery means that, with the minimum of movement, you can cover all the options available to your opponent, and that you should never be out of position for any stroke that you choose to execute.

Teaching tip: face the position to which you have hit the ball.

Anticipation

Anticipation is the ability to isolate the visual cues and so create more time to make decisions and execute a more forceful game.

The aim is to translate the information that

you see – i.e. what your opponent has done with the ball in the way of speed, spin and direction.

Be aware of your actions and the target (or targets) you have chosen, then watch your opponent's actions. His bat angle tells you the spin and speed, and where it is facing tells you the direction. After your opponent has struck the ball, watch it carefully for any irregularities. From a tactical point of view, try to work out what an opponent is capable of producing from certain targets that you have chosen, then play to those areas.

Teaching tip: watch your opponent and his bat after you have struck the ball. After your opponent makes contact, watch the ball.

Overall Balance

The questions that arise from table tennis produce no mystical answers. The long journey towards world class table tennis can only be produced with great effort from a

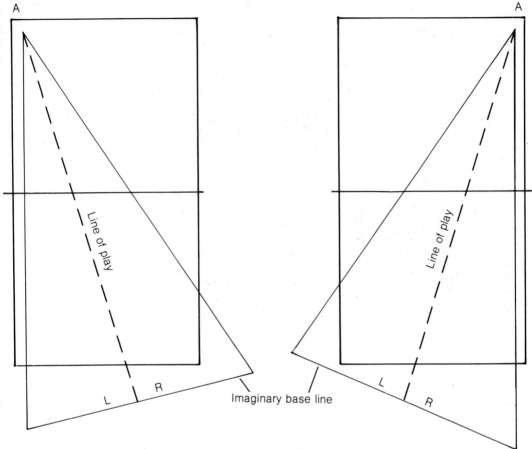

Fig 19   *Recovery: after playing the ball to target area A, recover to a position along the new imaginary base line. Left-handed players should move to the right so that their left foot is nearest to the line of play.*

whole host of people – officials; coaches; administrators; sports scientists; parents; practice partners and so on.

The efforts produced technically should have the basis of a good logical sequence of events to have any chance of achieving full potential. That sequence being:

Length – short.
Timing – peak.
Table position – close.
Base – square.
Body action – crouch.
Free arm – points.

Bat arm – shoulder; elbow; wrist.
Recovery.
Anticipation.

The system should be viewed as a balancing act: placed on the scales and weighed. If something is gained on one hand, something is lost on the other. The relationship that exists between all the technical items is paramount and so the exclusion of any one of those items proves detrimental to the overall picture; the picture being the complete player.

2 Early Stroke Play

Grip *(Figs 20 to 23)*

The grip is essential to early stroke play as it determines the angle of the bat which in turn determines:

1. The height of the ball.
2. The depth of the ball.
3. The speed of the ball.
4. The type of spin.
5. The amount of spin.

A good grip should be thought of as gentle for touch strokes and firm for speed and power. The index finger and thumb control touch, with a tightening of the three remaining for power.

The emphasis should be placed on the forefinger and thumb making contact with the blade of the bat, with the three remaining fingers gently surrounding the handle to increase stability. The shoulder of the bat should make slight contact with the area of the hand between the thumb and forefinger so that the bat becomes and feels like an extension of the hand. The grip should not be changed between backhand and forehand strokes.

Early stroke play should have a good mechanical base on which it can develop to its full potential. This will enable a style of play to develop which is both effective and economical in effort. A firm foundation adds up to good ball control.

Backhand Push *(Figs 24 to 28)*

A backhand push is essentially a holding stroke designed to discourage your opponent from attacking the ball vigorously.

Aim

The aim is to keep the ball low over the net and short enough for the ball to theoretically bounce twice on the receiver's side with the second bounce being as near as possible to the receiver's base line.

Method

Backhand pushes should be played with:

1. A short stroke.
2. A peak of bounce timing.
3. A close to the table position.
4. A square base.
5. A crouched posture.
6. A free hand pointing to the ball.
7. The elbow at ninety degrees on point of contact.

Tactical

To gain a good tactical advantage, push strokes should be used during the early part of the rally before it is forced to develop into faster flowing situations. Its purpose is to stop your opponent from gaining an advantage whilst creating an opening for yourself.

Teaching Tips

Try to make contact with the back bottom third of the ball using a slightly open bat angle (approximately forty-five degrees). This will allow the ball to be slowed suffi-

Fig 20   The shakehands grip – front view.

Fig 21   The shakehands grip – back view. Some players prefer to hold the bat without the forefinger running along the blade. This is called the hammer grip.

Fig 22 The pen grip – front view.

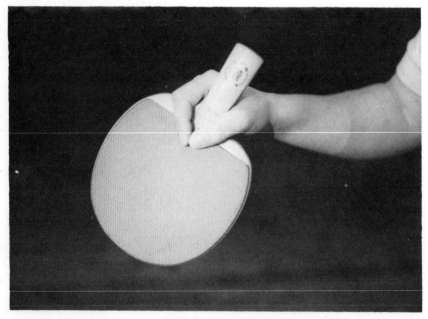

Fig 23 The pen grip – back view. There are several variations of the exact position of the fingers from splayed to just resting along the bat surface.

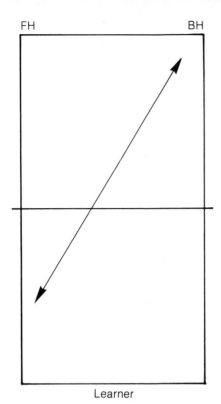

FH   BH

Learner

Fig 24   Practise the backhand push across
         the diagonal first.

Fig 25   Backhand push – preparation.

Fig 26   Contact.

Fig 27   Short follow-through.

17

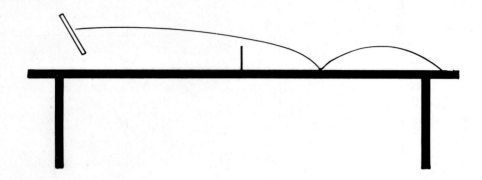

Fig 28 Backhand push exercise. In normal match play the ball is not allowed to bounce twice. This exercise is a guide for correct length.

ciently to achieve the target of two bounces on the receiver's side.

Forehand Drive *(Figs 29 to 32)*

Forehand drives are aggressive shots with the ingredient of: speed, spin and accuracy.

Aim

The aim is to force your opponent into an error situation by hitting the ball hard and deep. Its purpose should be to reduce your opponent's thinking time to an absolute minimum.

Method

1. Length should be short.
2. Timing – peak of bounce.
3. Close to the table position.
4. The base should be square to the line of play.

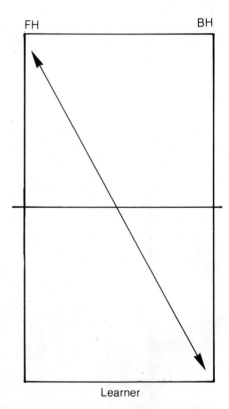

Fig 29 Forehand drive; playing along the diagonal gives you a longer distance and therefore an increased chance of success.

Fig 30   Preparation for a forehand drive.
Note how the free arm has moved
back parallel to the bat arm.

Fig 31   The ball has just been struck. Note
how the shoulder has come to the
front to provide the power.

Fig 32   The follow-through – as short as possible.

5. Crouched posture (quarter turn to right).
6. The free arm should point to the ball.
7. Bat arm – the stroke is produced from the shoulder (not the elbow or wrist).

Tactical

Drive strokes should be used at the earliest opportunity to maintain the maximum degree of pressure.

Teaching Tips

Practise holding the playing wrist with the free hand. This encourages hitting the ball at the most natural position in relation to the upper body whilst maintaining a good body turn to achieve power. Slowly bring the hands apart so that the overall rhythm of the stroke remains the same.

Backhand Drive *(Figs 33 to 36)*

A background drive is a speed stroke for attacking your opponent at the earliest opportunity.

Aim

Aim to probe for weaknesses in an opponent's game by speeding up the ball and forcing errors.

Method

1. Length should be short.
2. Timing – peak of bounce.
3. Close to the table position.
4. Square base.
5. Crouched posture.
6. The free arm points to the ball.
7. Bat arm – the stroke is produced from the elbow and wrist.

Tactical

Backhand drives are usually used either to impart or maintain speed on the ball. A ball which has speed can easily be returned with a degree of interest (i.e. with more speed).

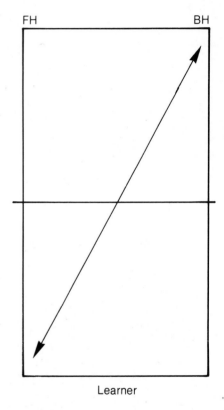

Fig 33 For the backhand drive again play along the diagonal.

Fig 34   Backhand drive – preparation.

Fig 35   Contact.

Fig 36   Follow-through.

Teaching Tips

Imagine you are throwing a 'frisbee'. The forward motion is produced from the elbow, the rotational effect comes from a wrist action. When striking on a backhand drive, try to get the point of contact between the bat and ball to be level with the elbow. The elbow acts as the power house. A major danger is that beginners try to use a shoulder action; the result being a lifting effect where a forward motion would be far more beneficial.

Forehand Push *(Figs 37 to 42)*

A forehand push is a safety stroke designed to probe for weaknesses in an opponent's armour.

Aim

Aim to keep the ball low and at a speed to enable the ball to bounce theoretically twice on the receiver's side. The second bounce should be directed to the opponent's base line. Usually, forehand pushes should have a degree of backspin.

Method

1. Length should be short.
2. Timing – peak of bounce.
3. Close to the table position.
4. Square base.
5. Crouched posture (quarter turn to right).
6. The free arm follows the direction of the ball.
7. Bat arm – the stroke is produced from the elbow.

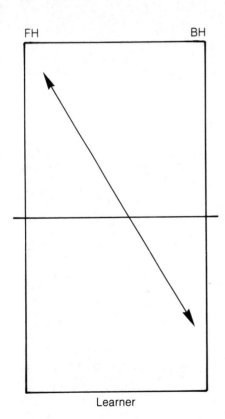

Fig 37   *Although the forehand push usually has a degree of backspin, current trends indicate that a stroke using a forward roll can be very effective.*

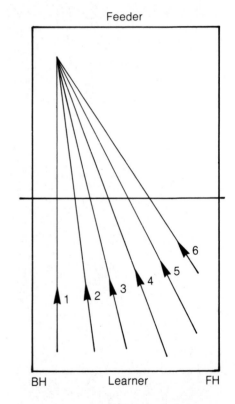

Fig 38   *Forehand push exercise; the pupil serves to the feeder who returns the ball to the areas indicated for the pupil to hit with a forehand push. When target 6 is completed, the feeder returns the ball to position 1 and repeats the sequence.*

Fig 39 Forehand push – preparation.

Fig 40 Just after contact.

Fig 41 Short follow-through in the direction
the ball is travelling. Many players
find this stroke difficult in their early
development, but regret its absence
from their game at higher levels.

Tactical

Forehand pushes should be played to probe
for weaknesses whilst keeping the ball very
safe. Vary the speed, spin and direction for
maximum advantage.

Teaching Tips

It is essential that there is space between the
upper arm and the body in a forward and
backward direction, not sideways. This,
linked with the crouched posture, allows you
to bring the elbow down offering a greater
range of bat angles with which to address the
ball. Encourage feeders to play the ball away
from you rather than directly to you, as this
helps you to achieve the space between arm
and body.

Fig 42 Forehand roll. This stroke is becoming more common, with the
bat commencing in the near
vertical position and using the
wrist to roll the bat over the ball.

Summary

These four simple strikes prove to be the base of all stroke play. They can be likened to a seed which is planted in the ground. Providing the right environment is maintained (coaching; practice; competition) the seed will grow at its own speed into whatever it is destined to be. Similarly the early strokes can grow into international level. Just as a seed grows into a plant, a stroke grows into control, speed and spin.

Service *(Figs 43 to 47)*

A simple service should be taught with the four basic strokes to enable a game to begin to develop at an early stage.

Short safety services can easily be developed from both backhand and forehand push strokes as the open angle of the bat provides a point of contact on the lower portion of the ball, making the ball move slowly and therefore short.

Aim

The aim is to keep the ball short, slow and low over the net to force the receiver into stretching forward to play the ball, thus losing a degree of control. A short service could be defined as one which would bounce at least three times on the receiver's side.

Method

Place the ball on the palm of the hand with the fingers together and the thumb free. Project the ball upwards to within forty-five degrees of a vertical position and strike on its downward path. All this should take place behind the base line or an extension of the base line and should remain within view of the umpire. At all times during the service action the bat

Open bat angle

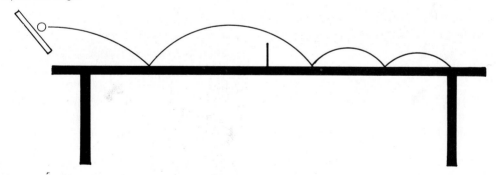

Fig 43   Short service; use a light touch and a slight downward brushing action. Do not try to 'knock' the ball onto the table.

Fig 44 A European International about to serve with a degree of sidespin added
for better effect. Note the concentration and body position.

should remain above the level of the table, and the point of contact should be between the receiver and some part of your body.

Tactical

Use a short service to bring the receiver in close to the net, forcing him to play at a stretch and provide a loose return.

Teaching Tips

There are a lot of rules and regulations which surround the service, so in the early stages of learning don't try to comply with all the regulations at once. Take things in easy stages:

1. Hold the ball between finger and thumb at

shoulder level and at a full arm's length, which will be approximately half-way down the table.

2. Hold the bat directly beneath the ball with a slightly open angle (about forty-five degrees) and just above net height.

3. Drop the ball onto the bat, maintaining the bat in a stationary position. The result will be that the ball will bounce off the bat onto the third of the table nearest the net on your own side, clearing the net and bouncing on the receiver's side.

4. Progressively drop the ball closer to your own base line until behind the base line. At each stage move the bat slightly forward in contact to maintain the first bounce close to the net.

5. When behind the base line place the ball in

Fig 45 A backhand sidespin service
just after the strike.

Fig 46 A forehand service with a high
throw.

the palm of the hand projecting it upwards about eighteen inches (half a metre). This allows time to co-ordinate the throwing and striking.

6. Choose the height of throw that is the easiest. A fast service could be produced from a backhand or forehand drive action following a similar progression to the short service. The difference in progression should be to drop the ball from behind the base line, striking so that the first bounce is half-way down the length of the table. With sufficient speed the ball will carry close to the receiver's base line.

Conclusions

Early stroke play should at every opportunity be thought of as integral components which need to be joined together into an overall rally situation.

Recovery is the process which will bind the various strokes into a complete rally. Every attempt should be made to appreciate how things are linked together; so, when working on early stroke play you should follow the pattern of:

1. Where is the ball to travel from? This will be either the position where your opponent is to serve from or the place you chose to play your last shot. This information should give you your starting position.
2. The nature of stroke you have chosen to play.
3. The target to which you have chosen to play the ball. This will determine the position to which you should recover.

Do not fall into the trap of thinking that because in practice you know the path the ball is supposed to travel, recovery becomes unnecessary. This only isolates the various strokes which under match conditions become inoperable. Rarely in a match do you know exactly where the ball will be

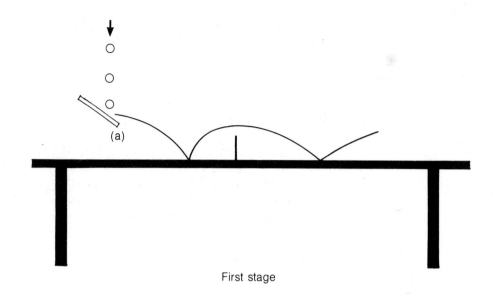

First stage

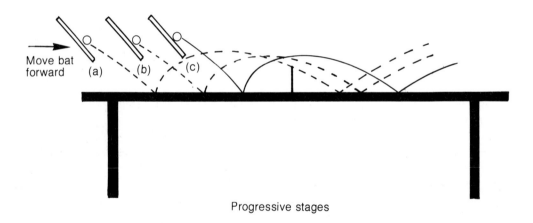

Move bat
forward   (a)   (b)   (c)

Progressive stages

Fig 47   Serving for beginners. Although this method of serving is not legal, it is temporarily accepted to enable the learner to get on with the basic instruction.

returned, so practice should reflect the options that would be available in a game situation.

The golden rule is: if it happens in a match, then practise it. If it does not happen in a match, then don't practise it.

Be aware, even in the early stages of development, of the bat actions of your opponent. This will provide essential information for your own actions.

3 Development of Style

GROWING PROCESS

Early stroke play grows into a style which has many governing factors; the main factor possibly being that of your physical and psychological make-up. Equipment and current fashions of other players' styles will also begin to affect your style. The development of new bat rubbers, blades that enhance or detract from the speed, spin and control are elements which have an effect on the tactical ploys used. These in turn affect the technical structure of how the game is played.

The 'growing process' follows the progression of: control – movement – speed and power – spin – anticipation.

Control

Control has to be considered as the starting point on the long hard road to success. Consider the system of nine points. The first four points are the machinery by which to control the ball or strokes in isolation. The seven points control the angles of the table, and nine points begin to control the opponent by forcing his options and reading his actions.

So control is viewed in early stages as:

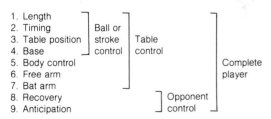

Movement (Fig 48)

Movement is the means to transport yourself and arrive in the most favourable position in which to execute the greatest range of strokes with maximum effectiveness and recover to a position from which to repeat the process.

Aim

The aim is to move in a balanced rhythmical way using as little effort as possible.

Method

Movement in table tennis terms can loosely be divided into three areas.

1. Footwork – area of base of body (position of the feet).
2. Body action – firstly the height of the body's centre of gravity; secondly the horizontal distance between the centre of gravity and either foot.
3. Arm movement – provides compensating adjustments.

Tactical

Footwork is required to move to the ball when your opponent plays it out of your reach. Footwork, body action and arm movement are necessary to strike the ball with the required effect, as it is body action which ultimately provides most of the power spin.

Teaching Tips

Concentrate on recovery when designing any exercise that requires specific movement. Recovery shows the starting points, the position and stroke production, the movement pattern and the position in which to finish. Try to keep the head at one level throughout all movement patterns. This helps to stabilise the body's balance, therefore assisting the body's flow.

Movement becomes the basis of all style; so it is imperative that a good rhythm and balance are achieved very early on. It is this good rhythm and balance which will determine the overall quality and effectiveness of the advanced techniques.

Fig 48 Fiona has moved across ready to attack the next ball. Note the wide stance and bent knee which will allow her to move in with speed and power.

Speed and Power *(Figs 49 & 50)*

Speed and power is the ability to make the ball travel quickly (directional force), spin (rotational force) or a combination of the two.

Aim

The aim is to hit the ball as hard as possible with as much spin as possible or a combination of the two. The thinking time of your opponent is greatly reduced, offering considerable advantage.

Method

This is achieved as a result of movement in the areas of footwork, body action and bat arm. It is therefore essential that general movement is acquired with good rhythm prior to attempting to strike a ball with speed and power.

When hitting a ball hard with a forehand stroke check that:

1. The weight transfers from one foot to the other (footwork).
2. The upper body turns to lengthen the approach to the ball, returning to a square position on execution (body action).
3. There is a pivot from the waist (body action).
4. The arm is accelerating on contact (bat arm).
5. The direction of the swing is in the same plane as the ball is to travel (bat arm).
6. The elbow joint is at approximately 120 degrees and points in the opposite direction to that in which the ball is to travel (bat arm).
7. The wrist is relaxed providing a slapping effect (bat arm).
8. Seventy per cent of the swing is before contact (bat arm).
9. The swing has a short follow-through

Fig 49 Forehand drive – early stage.

Fig 50 Forehand drive – follow-through position.

(thirty per cent of total) finishing with the bat pointing in the direction that the ball has travelled (bat arm).

Tactical

Speed and power strokes are best used following a slow ball as the contrast in speed presents problems to the receiver. They can, however, be played from any ball which has sufficient height.

Teaching Tips

It is important that speed and power strokes grow in balance with other strokes. A danger is for players in a practice situation to keep hitting one stroke harder and harder until the rally breaks down This will only isolate the technique from every other stroke and lose the overall aim of building rallies.

Speed Style *(Figs 51 & 52)*

A speed style of game is one where the player hits the ball with speed and power as opposed to spin.

Aim

The aim is to drive through the ball as early as possible to cut down the thinking and organisational time of the opponent. Taking the ball early widens the angle of target area available and also narrows the area available to the opponent. This narrowing means less movement is required, offering a considerable saving in time.

Method

Try, where possible, to use short sharp strokes travelling in a horizontal plane, striking the ball a fraction before the peak of the bounce. The ball should have sufficient height to be struck hard and yet be early enough to maximise the problems for the receiver.

A good square base to the line of play should be established with good recovery to reduce the angle of return, most of the power being generated from body turn and speed of arm.

Good anticipation skills are required to cope with the speed of play.

Tactical

A speed style of play is most effective against a spin style, especially a topspin player. Move the ball to many different targets on the table to upset the balance of your opponent. This will not necessarily stop him looping the ball, but will certainly dilute the speed and spin he is capable of producing. Against a backspin player, the only change that needs to be made is to change the angle of swing into more of an upward direction to compensate for the backspin effect of the ball pulling downwards. Producing speed strokes has a neutralising effect on the spin that exists on the ball. So exude an air of confidence and hit the ball hard.

Teaching Tips

Good hand to eye co-ordination skills are essential to a speed game, as are fast reflex actions. Concentrate efforts on just before peak bounce timing and relaxed wrist skills.

Fig 51   Speed style about to strike with full power.

Fig 52   Speed style – follow-through. Note the power generated through the forward movement and the shoulder coming through to the front.

Fig 53   A European International in action.

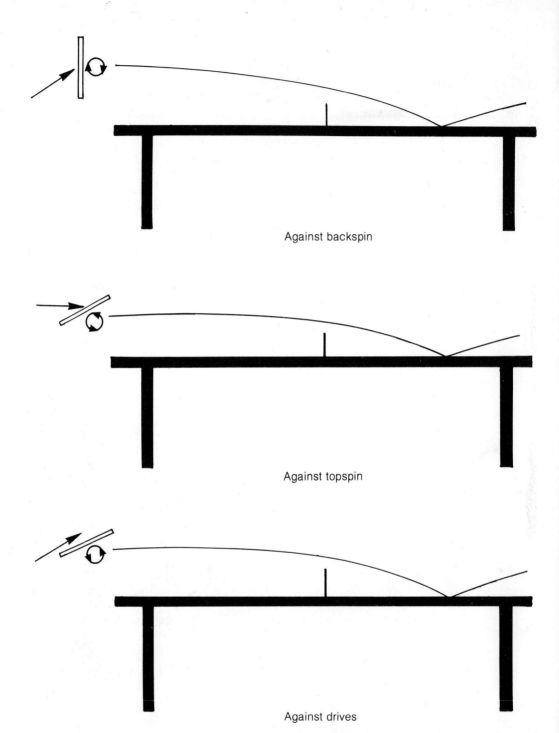

Against backspin

Against topspin

Against drives

Fig 54   Guidelines for playing against different styles. (These are only
         guidelines – the actual angles depend on the degree of spin
         placed on the ball by the opponent.)

Topspin Style

The topspin style is possibly the most common style in table tennis today, but is not necessarily the easiest to perform. It is a style in which the player brushes against the flight of the ball to produce spin.

Aim

The aim is to produce spin in varying degrees and at different speeds. A lot of spin produces mistakes through a breakdown in the control level of the opponent.

Method

The main spin producing factors are the speed of bat brushing against the flight of the ball with a light degree of touch at the right angle.

The most effective timing point is at the peak of the bounce. Don't fall into the trap of thinking it is possible to produce extra spin by letting the ball drop. This will only result in a loss of speed, whilst the spin remains the same.

Attempt to lengthen the playing arm slightly to approximately 100 to 110 degrees to gain a better acceleration on contact with the ball. Above all, recognise the spin nature of the ball approaching. This should tell you the angle of bat and swing to adopt.

Tactical

When using topspin against a speed player, use a slower first opening ball which has a higher trajectory. This will buy a little time to organise your own movements especially if you have played a long ball down the middle of the table or to your opponent's playing hip (cross over point), which will reduce the angle available to your opponent. The initial slow ball should then be followed by a faster topspin, usually to a different target.

Against another topspin player, it is wise to hold your ground quite close to the table and attempt to get your topspin in first or reply to his opening ball as forcefully as possible.

The overall balance is between maximum speed and spin to gain the best result. Watch your opponent's actions carefully. Remember, this will give you the information you require.

Backspin players present many problems for topspin players, possibly because the ball comes much slower and holds in the air much longer. This additional time in the air makes it difficult for the natural attacker to orientate himself to the approaching ball. Try, as a first line of attack, to fast spin and drive natural choppers. If that does not work

Fig 55 The ball has been played to the crossover point, forcing Alan to move awkwardly in order to execute his next shot.

35

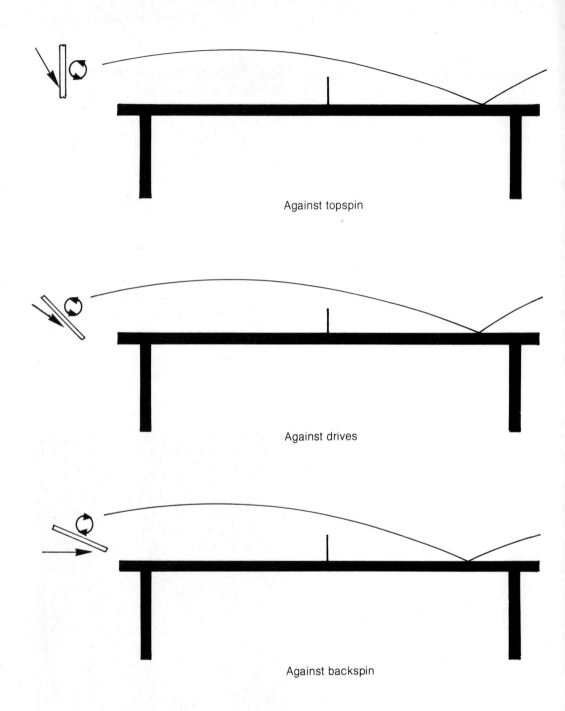

Against topspin

Against drives

Against backspin

Fig 56   *Peak of bounce timing should be used against drives and topspins,*
but a later timing can sometimes be advantageous to gain a
better trajectory. However, you should always play a backspin
ball at the top of the bounce.

then be very patient and slow loop until you create the higher return ready for a fast loop or smash. Build up down the middle of the table or to the playing hip (cross over point), then drive wide to either corner.

Teaching Tips

Emphasise that the finger and thumb are the main contributing factors concerning the grip of the bat when learning spin strokes. Relax the wrist joint as much as possible as this helps to accelerate the bat on contact to gain maximum spin.

Develop topspin strokes as an extension of drive strokes, allowing the spin to grow naturally when the subtle changes in bat angle, swing angle and the degree of touch lessen. The rhythm of movement should remain the same as the speed style to gain the best overall result of deception. If one type of stroke is produced in the same way as another then the skill level is potentially higher and the opponent has less information by which to assess the nature of ball produced.

Backspin Style *(Figs 57 to 61)*

Backspin style produces backspin in varying degrees. It should be viewed as attacking the ball not defending.

Aim

The overall aim is to force your opponent into misreading the backspin, so forcing an error. Vary the speed and depth to interrupt your opponent's natural flow.

Method

Backspin is produced in just the same way as topspin, so the angles of swing and bat plus the degree of touch are crucial to the

brushing effect to gain spin. There may be occasions where it is advantageous to allow the ball to go slightly past the peak of the bounce; remember that this will forfeit the speed but can aid a better trajectory. The lack of speed allows gravity to take a greater effect to bring the ball down to the playing surface. Use a later timing only against a ball which has speed or topspin. A ball with backspin should always be played at the top of the bounce.

Tactical

Use backspin against speed and topspin players to slow the general play down and to buy extra time. Receives of serves are sometimes too difficult to impart speed and topspin, so use a lot of backspin to keep your opponent from opening the rally with great force.

Fig 57 Backspin style - ready position.

Fig 58 Peak of bounce timing.

Fig 59 Delayed timing.

Teaching Tips

The emphasis is on grip, with the finger and thumb on the blade of the bat. Use a relaxed wrist. In early stages don't be frightened of producing a high ball, and concentrate on acquiring a good drag effect between bat and ball.

Fig 60 Follow-through.

Fig 61   Jill Hammersley-Parker, for many years the Women's No. 1 in
England, and a great exponent of the backspin style.

4 Development of Match Play

Service

Service is the first stroke to occur in any rally; it is the means by which to introduce the rally.

Aim

The aim is to put your opponent under pressure and the service should be viewed as the first link in the chain towards winning a point. If the service is good then the follow-up stroke will be easier. If the service is bad then the opportunity to develop the advantage is limited.

To attack a service the receiver needs height and/or depth: height to be able to hit the ball hard; depth to spin it heavily. So these two components should be removed from short service techniques. A good attacking service would be one where the ball bounces on the receiver's side twice, with the second bounce on the base line. This should be short enough to stop the receiver attacking with great force, but long enough to provoke a deeper return to enable the server to attack.

Method (Figs 62 & 63)

To gain maximum advantage, the second bounce on the receiver's side should be on the base line. To achieve this, the bounce on the server's side should be between halfway and two-thirds of the way down his side of the table.

The contact on the ball, the direction of

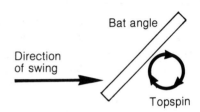

Bat angle

Direction of swing

Topspin

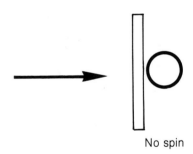

No spin

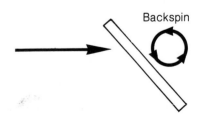

Backspin

Fig 62   The contact on the ball, direction of serving and bat angle will determine the spin.

40

serving and the angle of the bat will determine the spin.

The height of contact will be determined by the nature of spin produced. Topspin has a tendency to bounce a little lower than backspin, so the height of contact should be adjusted accordingly.

Tactical (Figs 64 & 65)

From a tactical point of view relax the grip as much as possible to allow a greater degree of flexibility in the wrist. The greater the range of wrist movement, the easier it becomes to build in deception. Different areas of the bat surface travel in different directions. Thus, by changing the point of contact on the bat blade, different types and degrees of spin can be achieved. The ball also offers a wide range of points of contact, which again gives numerous variations.

Remember that backspin and sidespin, and topspin and sidespin blend together.

Select your service position as carefully as you would your target, as the position of the ball determines the target available to the receiver.

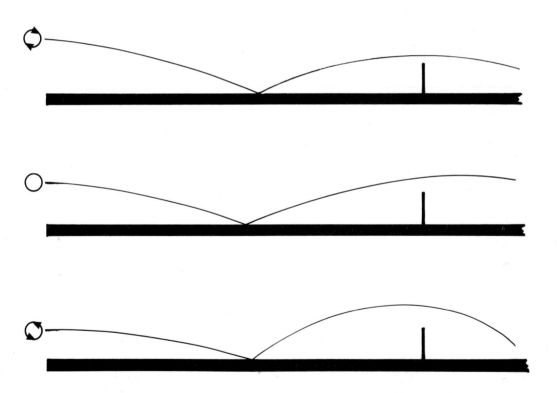

Fig 63   The height of contact will be determined by the nature of spin produced.

Development of Match Play

Teaching Tips

Learn to drag the ball across the bat with a loose wrist when the spin is acquired, then concentrate on the positioning. In the service, it is usually necessary to watch the ball until it is much closer to the bat than in other strokes, to enable a finer degree of touch to be achieved.

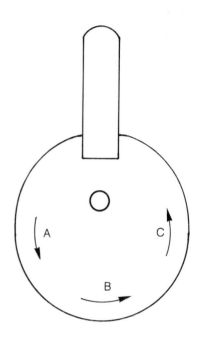

Fig 64 (right) By moving the wrist in a circular manner it is possible to impart different spins to the ball, because each area of the bat is travelling in a different direction. Thus, in a backhand service, a ball struck by point A would produce a clockwise sidespin, by point B a backspin, and by point C an anticlockwise sidespin.

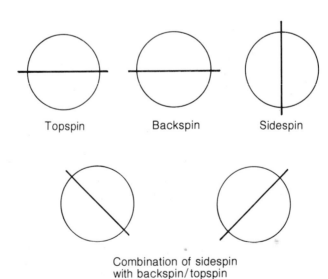

Topspin   Backspin   Sidespin

Combination of sidespin with backspin/topspin

Fig 65 The wide range of points of contact give variations of spin.

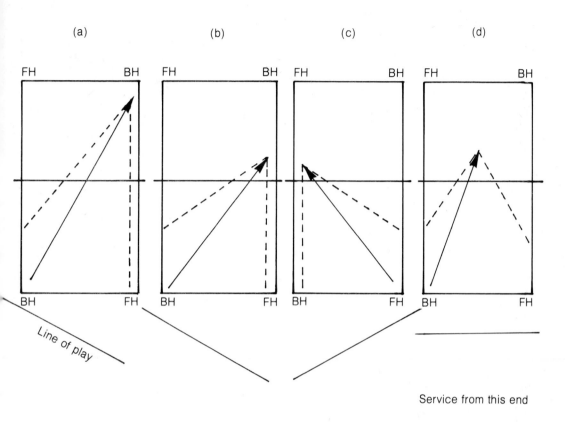

(a)   (b)   (c)   (d)

FH   BH   FH   BH   FH   BH   FH   BH

BH   FH   BH   FH   BH   FH   BH   FH

Line of play

Service from this end

Fig 66   Having made your service, your stance should be taken up along the appropriate line of play.

Receive of Service

For many people the receive of service holds numerous traps; sometimes, for example, it is very difficult to read the variations of spins. It should be understood that there is nothing mystical about service and the spins produced; service returns, therefore, are equally straightforward.

Aim

Try to attack the ball if possible; view the service receive as the first opportunity to make a winner. Be decisive and have the courage of your convictions by being positive.

When choosing a receive stroke, put them in the following order:

1. Smash.
2. Fast loop.
3. Slow loop.
4. Wrist flick.
5. Fast heavy push.
6. Slow heavy push.
7. Short touch.

Fig 67 *Service position for doubles. The use of a high throw imparts more spin.*

Fig 68 *Service showing the amount of drag about to be imparted on the ball. Note the loose wrist.*

Thus, for example, if it is not possible to return the ball using a smash, consider a fast loop; if this is not possible a slow loop and so on.

Method

Remember that a ball can only revolve around one central axis. If, by watching the server's bat action carefully, you know the direction of that spin, there will be three options open to you to overcome the spin:

1. To play with the spin – keeping the ball revolving in the same direction.
2. To neutralise the ball – take the spin off.
3. To reverse the direction of the ball – make the ball rotate in the opposite direction.

The easiest course of action is possibly to neutralise the ball by simply facing the bat in

44

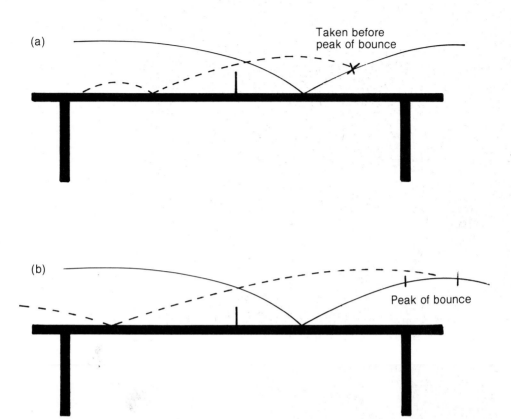

(a)   Taken before peak of bounce

(b)   Peak of bounce

Fig 69   (a) Short returns; (b) attacking returns.

the direction of where the server's action starts. This will normally, if a light but positive touch is used in a forward direction, return the ball to approximately the centre of the table. However, there are drawbacks in that this presents few problems for the server.

Think of your normal service actions and use them in a receive situation. Give the server more to worry about by producing a heavily spun ball. If your bat speed brushing against the ball is greater than the rotation on the ball, then the spin has little or no effect.

Tactical

By striking the ball as near as possible to or on its central axis, the spin on the ball has little effect. For example, if the server uses only sidespin on his service, a heavy topspin or backspin stroke would prove easy to execute and have good effect. Whereas a topspin or backspin service could easily be countered with sidespin.

If your bat speed is great and you have good touch skills, consider going with the spin and keep the ball turning on the same axis and in the same direction. For example, if the server serves with backspin and the ball is deep enough, impart heavy topspin and allow the spin already on the ball to assist you.

Many players choose to reverse the spin, especially returning backspin with backspin or topspin with topspin. The trick here is to first neutralise the existing spin by setting the angle of the bat open against backspin, closed against topspin, and then impart your own chosen spin.

In your mind, choose as early as possible the nature of your receive stroke. Choose the timing point according to the type of receive you wish to play. If you choose to play the ball as short as possible, then strike the ball as early as possible after the bounce. This will allow you the shortest route to your chosen target and allow you the greatest degree of accuracy. If you choose a more ambitious receive, allow the ball to rise to its highest point where a greater range of strokes and targets are available to you because of the greater angle.

Teaching Tips

Have your practice partner use his strongest services constantly, and experiment with different types of receive. Don't be frightened to attack the ball, as courage not recklessness usually pays dividends.

Loops *(Figs 70 to 76)*

Loop Drives

Loop drives produce very heavy topspin. The aim is to produce heavy spin with the best option on speed.

Fig 70 Loop drive – preparation.

Fig 71 Follow-through.

Fig 72 Loop drive against chop. Note the near vertical bat.

Fig 73 Loop drive against chop, after contact.

Loop v Chop

The length of stroke can be a little longer than with an ordinary drive, although care must be taken to ensure that the greater part of the swing is before the point of contact between bat and ball. Where possible, hit the ball at the top of its bounce to ensure the best angle towards the target area.

All spin and power and speed strokes originate in the feet, so push hard with the legs allowing the movement to pass through the body from almost a sitting position to a standing position.

Use a near vertical bat angle with a slightly arcing direction of the swing moving slightly over the ball. The more backspin on the ball, the more vertically the swing should travel.

Loop v Loop

Again the stroke originates in the feet with a push from the back to the front foot, in a forward direction. The bat angle must be fairly closed, with the swing travelling quickly in a near horizontal direction. There should be a great deal of upper body turn to help greater bat speed.

Tactical

Loop drives can be used in all attacking situations when the ball has sufficient depth to enable the bat to travel in an upward direction without the table being an obstruction.

Fig 74 *Loop drive against loop.*

Teaching Tips

Roll the ball off the end of the table to establish a good rhythm of movement and good contact between bat and ball.

Half-volley Blocking
(Figs 77 & 78)

A block requires very little bat movement and therefore needs speed or spin from the opponent. The more the opponent does with the ball, the less you need to do with a block shot.

The key is to set the angle of the bat to achieve the best rebound effect, facing the target to which you wish the ball to travel. Think of block shots as a means of returning an opponent's aggression. Strike the ball as early as possible to cut thinking and organisational time down. Do as little as possible with the bat, allowing the ball to bounce back.

Fig 75 *Loop drive – preparation below the table with bat angle closed.*

Fig 76 *Loop drive – follow-through showing bat angle and short stroke.*

Fig 77 Half-volley block – at contact.

Fig 78 Half-volley block – after contact.

High Defence *(Figs 79 & 80)*

High defence can be used when all else fails. If you are under pressure, you have to buy time and so return the ball very high.

Try to get the ball as high as possible to increase your recovery time, putting as much topspin on the ball as possible. The topspin will send the ball forwards after its bounce, forcing the receiver into playing the ball further back from the table.

Think of the technique as a very high loop shot. Try to get a good push from the legs and a very fast arm action. Use when under great pressure against a smash or very fast loop.

Kill Shot

The kill shot should never come back. The ball should be played with extreme force to the biggest available space.

Think of the technique as a very hard drive with a much greater commitment of the body weight. The total body weight must travel in the same direction as the ball is to travel using every ounce of energy. At least eighty per cent of the swing should be before the point of contact to achieve the maximum degree of acceleration and force.

Use against high returns when you are sure of the situation.

Fig 79 *High defence giving the ball good height and added topspin.*

Fig 80 *The ball has been placed high and to the edge of the table, with a good degree of topspin making it kick off the surface. The player, caught out of position, must attempt to reach the ball.*

Fig 81   A drop shot, showing the bat angle open to combat the backspin
that is on the ball.

Counterhit

The counterhit is used when the approaching ball has good speed, and returns it with speed.

Hit the ball as early as possible after the bounce, with the shot travelling in a horizontal direction using a relaxed wrist producing a slapping effect. Always use a square base with upper body turn to help produce additional speed.

A shot most effective against drive and topspin style players.

Drop Shot *(Fig 81)*

This shot should be used when the opponent has been forced away from the table. The shot is made with as little spin and speed as possible so that the ball travels only a short distance.

Time the ball as early as possible with a very relaxed wrist. The important factor is to take all the speed out of the ball. A drop shot is especially effective against defensive players.

5 Coaching and Training Practice

SKILLS AWARDS

Skills Awards in table tennis can vary around the world, but in general they have been developed as a means to provide incentives for young players to practise systematically.

Skills Awards generally take the form of a series of tests to be performed to a stated standard. There are usually several grades to cater for all people from beginners to top league players. The tests are supervised, players reaching the standard required can obtain a badge and certificate from the appropriate Table Tennis Association.

As the main instigator of the first National Award Scheme in England during the 1960s following months of trials, I believe that the spin-off effects of Awards Schemes are also of great value to the sport. They can be applied to judge a coach's own degree of skill, whilst for teachers they provide a means to arrange self-governing groups (pupil, controller and critic) so that several tables can be in action in a completely organised and efficient way.

The aim of Skills Awards is to provide an incentive to young players in particular to practise systematically, and to act as an introduction to tactical play and build a framework of disciplined play for all levels of players.

To find out details of Awards Schemes write to the International Table Tennis Federation or to your National Association who will immediately send you copies of the rules and details of tests involved. In England the Awards Scheme that I recommend is operated in a joint venture by the English Table Tennis Association and the English Schools Table Tennis Association on behalf of the Dunlop Sports Company. There are five grades: One, Two, Three, Matchplayer and Master.

The use of Skills Awards exercises has proved very beneficial to many current top players. They provide a solid foundation for control whilst keeping interest levels high, and offer a logical development of play.

'To fail to prepare, prepare to fail', says the adage; the use of Skills Awards avoids this danger.

PRACTICE

Practice is the repetition of a particular stroke, sequence or situation, with the aim of making that stroke, sequence or situation become an automatic reflex action. In other words, the aim is to be able to perform the action instinctively, reducing the amount of thinking to the minimum level possible. The reason for this is that thinking about how an action is to be performed slows the execution down drastically and also allows more time for your opponent.

Method

Where possible try to practise at three levels:

1. With people of a higher standard so that

you can learn new tricks.

2. With people of the same standard in order to get your tactics right.

3. With people of a lower standard to enable you to create gaps in an opponent's game.

It is not always possible to find players willing to practise with a purpose, but this should be a prime objective. If and when you do, divide up the time available equally and allow your partner to choose his own exercises for the period.

If you are playing against weaker players, you can put yourself under some form of pressure to increase the effectiveness of the practice. For example:

1. Take all balls with your backhand regardless of where they are played to. This will put pressure on footwork and correct body positioning.

2. Invent difficult tasks by considering small target areas. These can be marked by sheets of paper.

Remember that half an hour of concentrated practice is worth at last three hours of aimless knocking up.

There are three main areas of practice: technical, tactical and physical training.

Technical

This area deals with strokes and footwork patterns to ensure that they work well under the pressures of a match situation. It is here that corrections should be made in faulty strokes and movements.

Most of the technical section should be carried out in the off-peak season when a degree of physical fitness has also been achieved. Technical practice requires a degree of co-operation from your practice partner. Initially, until the movement pattern is comfortable and can be reproduced with an easy rhythm, you should ask for simple and set returns. Once you feel you have established an easy rhythm ask your partner to increase the pressure from his end to bring the situation nearer to that of a match play.

Practice should cover the complete range of bat angles from an open angle to a closed (chopping against chop to looping against loop). Your style of game should tell you the ratio. Have a set routine of practices that cover the complete range of angle skills.

Imagine a scale of nought to one hundred, nought being a total novice and one hundred being the current World Champion. Everybody would fall somewhere on the scale; do not try to copy the World Champion's techniques, but work progressively towards one hundred. To imitate certain strokes of the internationals leaves big gaps in your game; study the internationals to see how they engineer the opportunity to use their big strokes rather than just seeing the strokes.

Tactical

This practice is designed to give you an edge over any opponent in general or, when carried out prior to a specific match, a given or named player.

Tactical practice should be adopted during the final run into the main competitive part of your year, as well as during the period.

Physical Training

In order to carry out any extensive technical and tactical programme you will need to maximise your body's physical capabilities. This can be done as a private venture, but I consider that a small group of keen players meeting on a regular basis will achieve a more disciplined approach by applying pressure on all to compete and attend.

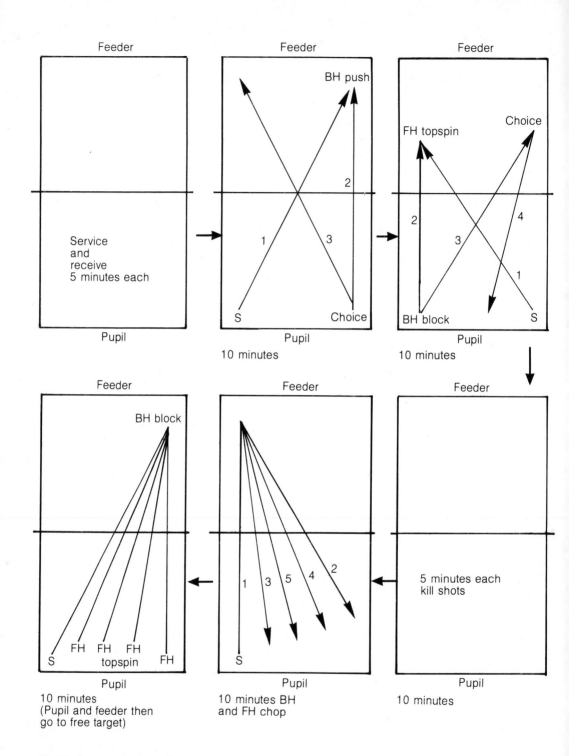

Fig 82 *Suggested scheme for a six table practice session.*

Extent of Practice

I have often been asked what should be the proportion of practice to match play. Serious international players practise for up to six hours each day; this is not counting the physical training programme. Too many players allow demands on their available time to interfere with this important side of their game. Each ball struck in practice should be thought of as twenty-five pence in the bank so that in a match situation there is enough experience and ability to draw from. Each ball struck in your highest level of competition costs you £1.00. Try to reach a ratio of four hours of practice to one hour of match play.

Teaching Tips

No player reaches any level without the help of others, so respect your partners and be prepared to help others in a similar way.

When practising, start each rally with a service and receive so that it remains in the context of a match situation.

Off the table exercises with bat and ball can be used to develop touch and spin, and the results of your actions can be quickly learned by following the procedure of:

1. Using the forehand side only, bounce the ball to a height no more than one foot (30cm). Gradually start to impart sidespin in the same direction. The more spin and the longer the practice can be maintained, the better.
2. As previous exercise, but the opposite sidespin.
3. Right-handed players spin the ball from right to left and then set an angle of approximately forty-five degrees to neutralise the spin on the ball. Alternate with spin and neutralise.

4. Spin the ball alternately right to left and then left to right.

Note: the ball should bounce near to the vertical at all times.

FITNESS

Physical fitness means the overall physical condition of a person. For table tennis it can be broken down into sections: speed, agility, strength and endurance.

Speed Training (Reaction Time)

Speed is the time taken to co-ordinate the movements of the individual joints or the body as a whole. As a player you are required to use your brain, eyes, hands, waist, legs and feet simultaneously within a split second, and this action is repeated, according to the length of the rally, several times in succession. Whilst reaction time can be reduced by both technical and tactical practices so that actions become autonomous, the body must be physically capable at the same time.

Exercises for speed should include:

1. Short runs of no more than fifty metre lengths.
2. Change direction runs (this means that the trainer changes your direction by random command).

Agility Training *(Figs 84 to 91)*

Agility depends upon flexibility of movement of a joint or a series of joints in the body, and the co-ordination of reaction time and strength.

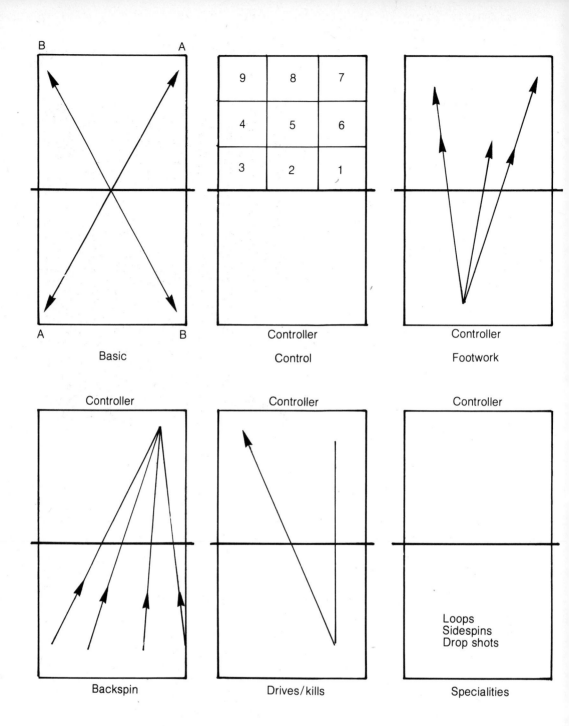

B   A

A   B

Basic

9	8	7
4	5	6
3	2	1

Controller

Control

Controller

Footwork

Controller

Backspin

Controller

Drives/kills

Controller

Loops
Sidespins
Drop shots

Specialities

Fig 83   *A suggested scheme for a six table rally. When organising a rally, keep the sessions interesting by moving the players through a variety of practices. Change each exercise every thirty minutes in order to keep up the concentration levels. Select the right coach for the right table practice.*

Exercises for agility should include:

1. *Rope skipping* This exercise helps not only jumping ability but the co-ordination between arm and leg movement. The session should be commenced with five minutes of steady skipping using an alternate foot action and adding variations such as jumping off both feet with the rope moving round the body first once and then twice. Conclude with a fast skipping routine of thirty seconds; rest for two minutes and repeat five times.

2. *High jumps* If there is equipment available, try to improve your previous height record over six attempts per session. If not, stand upright with your feet together and jump as high as you can into the air. Repeat the exercise at a steady pace for thirty seconds; rest for two minutes and repeat four times.

3. *Long jumping* This is best carried out with a long jump pit to prevent damage to ankles or feet. Always try to beat your best previous mark in order to extend muscle movement.

4. *Trunk swings* Stand upright with feet slightly apart. Place arms straight out from body in front of you and commence a pattern of swinging them from left to right, moving as much as possible from the waist. Try limbering up by simple side to side movements of the upper body from the waist only and then finish the exercise routine by carrying out a series of dummy forehand topspin drives. These simulated off-the-table stroke practices (often called *shadow play*) are invaluable to players unable to fit in the amount of table practice but who wish to keep their bodies in peak condition for the game.

5. *Cycling in the air* I believe that going out for a fast five mile cycle ride each week will assist the flexibility of the legs and that cycling generally is a good exercise for any

Fig 84   Rope skipping.

athlete. However, as a daily routine you can simulate the cycling pattern by lying face-up on the floor, lifting your legs and lower trunk into the air and balancing with your elbows pressing on the floor. Commence a cycling action with your legs and keep up a fast thirty second exercise, followed by a two minute break. Repeat four times.

6. *Knee circling* This exercise loosens up the knee joints and keeps them supple. Stand upright and adopt a table tennis ready position with knees bent. Commence a circling action of the knees, first clockwise for two minutes and then anticlockwise.

7. *Full arm swings* Stand upright. Start this routine by throwing your arms backwards and then forwards with shoulders back. Then commence full arm circling with both arms moving in the same direction, then alternate to the arms moving in opposite directions.

Fig 85 Trunk swings - commencement.

Fig 86 Trunk swings - finish.

Fig 87 Cycling in the air.

The idea is to loosen up the muscles in the shoulders which play such an important role in table tennis. Continue for five minutes.

8. *Wrist flexing* Place both hands out in front of you with your elbows bent at ninety degrees. Bend the wrists downwards to a maximum position and then commence a circling action of the wrists, first one way and then the other. The object is to build a firm but supple wrist to allow flexibility for flicks and speed shots. This exercise should always be carried out just before playing to loosen up and remove any stiffness that there might be from such activities as driving or motor bike riding.

Fig 88   Knee circling - commencement.

Fig 89   Knee circling in progress.

Fig 90   Full arm swings.

Fig 91   Wrist flexing.

Fig 92   Push-ups - ready position.

Fig 93   Note that when lowering to the floor the whole body is in a
straight line, with no sagging in the middle.

Strength Training
(Figs 92 to 100)

This area must be carefully monitored, as weight lifting or exercises using tension springs will tend to make muscles thick or stiff at the cost of speed.

Exercises should include:

1. *Push-ups* (men only)   Sometimes called press-ups. Lie face-down on the floor, with your hands palm down and level with your chest. Push your body upwards until your arms are fully outstretched. Hold your head, trunk and legs in a straight line without any sag. Next, lower the arms until they are bent,

Fig 94   One-handed push-ups.

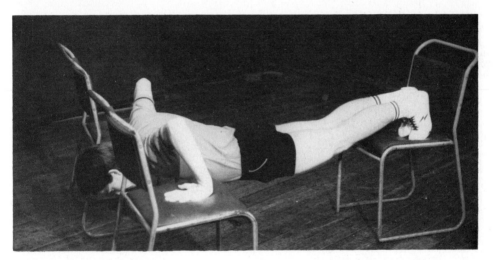

Fig 95   Push-ups using chairs.

but without allowing the body to touch the floor. When you reach a position where your chest is three inches off the ground, push upwards once more. Repeat the exercise until you reach a point of discomfort. Players vary in the amount of push-ups they can achieve, but practice usually extends the number if repeated over a period of time. Those who find it easy can try the following: one arm press-ups (keeping one hand behind your back); extension press-ups (with arms placed out in front of your head); and press-ups with the feet resting on a bench or similar object.

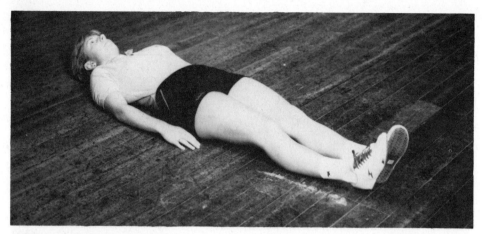

Fig 96 *Ready position for sit-ups.*

Fig 97 *Touch your toes if possible.*

2. *Dips* These require the use of a parallel bar, but can be done by resting the hands on two secured chairs. Balance above the bars with your arms straight, then bend your arms to an angle of ninety degrees at the elbow. Keep the feet off the floor for the entire exercise. See how many you can complete and gradually increase the number. *Do not* push yourself beyond the pain barrier.

3. *Sit-ups* Lie on the floor face-up and stretch out with your hands by your side. Sit up and touch your toes with your hands. Repeat for two minutes. A variation on this is to get a partner to hold your feet (or place them under a low bed or chair) so that your feet don't lift off the floor. Stretch your hands out above your head, sit up and touch your toes, repeating the exercise for two minutes.

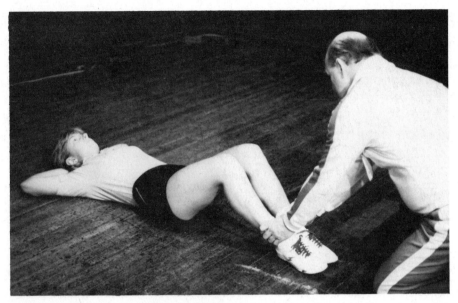

Fig 98   Sit-up variation which exercises the stomach muscles to the maximum. Ready position with knees bent and hands behind head.

Fig 99   Sit-up variation, completing the movement by touching elbows on knees.

4. *Jumping over benches* Keep your feet together and jump sideways over a bench or similar obstacle about 25cm high. Immediately on landing, jump back again to the other side. Keep up this side-to-side movement for as long as you reasonably can.

Endurance Training

For table tennis this means the ability to continue physical activity throughout any required match or tournament period. The object of endurance is therefore to reduce the risk of fatigue. As fatigue sets in, the reaction time becomes slower and muscles lose their flexibility; this appears as a breakdown in agility.

Exercises should include:

1. Jogging (gradually extending distance and time).
2. Interval running (this consists of running a specified number of short distances in a given time).
3. Training. Jogging five minutes, running five minutes, walking five minutes, skipping five minutes, jogging five minutes and so on.

Note: all these exercises should be carried out together with a qualified instructor who will be able to set guidelines and standards for you to match.

Warm-up Activities

It has been common practice for years to recommend that players warm up before playing in matches. Various standards have been set down and many people will continue to write on this subject. As I see it, the purpose of a warm-up session is for each player to be at the top of his physical and mental capability when he walks to the table.

I have already written about physical

Fig 100   Jumping over an object for as long and as fast as you can.

warming-up as a personal strategy. As a group session I would also recommend some simple routines such as:

1. Running around the hall slowly.
2. Running backwards.
3. Running side to side.
4. Running and jumping high in the air.
5. Body flexing: arms, legs, feet and wrists.
6. Off the table stroke reproduction.

The most important warm-up, however, is not with the body but in the mind. This is the area least considered by the majority, with the exception of the Asian players.

Each person has different arousal levels: some too high and some often too low. This is where your coach really comes in; he should be able to understand your moods and your innermost thoughts. By revealing to him your fears and ambitions, he should be able to decide what your driving force consists of and how best to use it. This complete communication system established between you will, when perfected, produce a much higher rate of success as long as you put your full trust in him and respect his judgement. As you progress to the top you may have to change your adviser for a coach or trainer more skilled in other subjects. At this change, you will both need time to adjust to varying personality and communication problems.

FUN GAMES

Purpose

For many years now, table tennis coaches have introduced a fun element into their training sessions. This helps to keep the concentration level of their pupils on a high note whilst still serving as a valuable practice period.

The following are some suggestions for fun games.

French Table Tennis (Fig 101)

This involves a group of players who space themselves equally around the table. Each player makes a stroke and then runs to the other end. When a player fails to make a good return he drops out. This continues until there are only two players left; one point is then played and the winner counts one to his score. The game starts again until the first person to reach eleven points is declared the winner.

There are variations to this game:

1. Players play in pairs.

2. Only push play or positional play is allowed.
3. Obstacles are placed in the way of the circuit, or the players have to jump over benches or touch the back walls before coming to the table.
4. The last two players have to turn around one full circle after making each stroke.

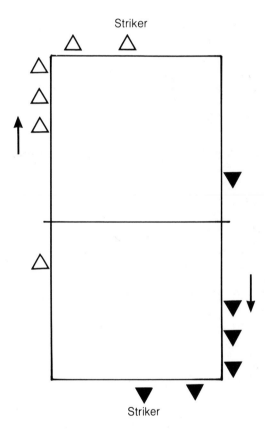

Fig 101 French table tennis. This game is very useful where there is an excess of people for the number of tables available.

Bat Edge

The ball is played first on the blade of the bat then on the edge. The number of successes is scored in three attempts.

Minute Rally

Two players per team; the number of strokes that two players can achieve in one minute is counted.

Variations of the game include the naming of different strokes or combinations of strokes.

Badminton

Points are only won by the server. The person who wins the toss commences serving. Thereafter, it is the winner of the previous point who serves. Play eleven points for a win.

Football (Fig 102)

In teams of two, a pair play the ball to each other across the diagonal. One player sees his opportunity and smashes the ball down the line. If the opposition fails to return the ball, a goal is scored. Alternate services.

Golf

Players serve into random placed buckets or receptacles. Variations include:

1. Use of short, medium and long positions for bounce.
2. A player is nominated as the attacking player and has to hit the ball twice before trying to place a drop shot into a receptacle placed just over the net. A set number of points is played, after which the second player attempts the exercise. The winner is the one achieving the most bucketed shots.

Reverse

Players have to strike the ball so that it hits their side of the table before travelling over the net.

Piggy Back Singles

The game is played in teams of two with one player on the back of another. A change is made after each point. Variations include:

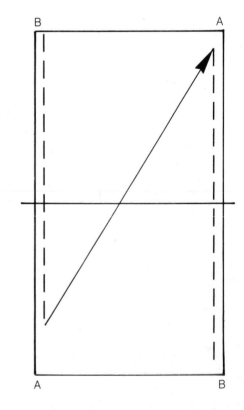

Fig 102   Football; team B are waiting for a smash.

1. Groups of players at each end.
2. Players change only when a point is lost.

Warning: beware of differences in weight that could cause injury.

Team Singles

Minimum of two per team. When a player loses a point only that player is replaced. Twenty-one points for the winner.

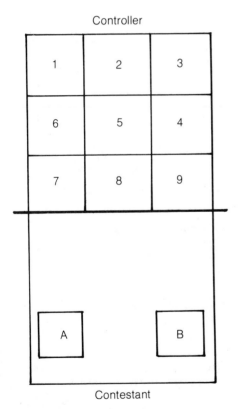

Controller

Fig 103   Numbers; be careful not to scratch the table with the chalk.

Overtaking

The players sprint around the gymnasium with the ball balanced on the bat. If overtaken or if they drop the ball, they drop out of the game.

Numbers (Fig 103)

One side of a table is divided into nine sections using a piece of string and chalk. Each section is numbered from one to nine. The coach calls out the number for the opponent to play to. The number of accurate strikes is counted for each player within five minutes.
Variations include:

1. The player under test has to play to each section in turn. The number of accurate strikes within either a time period or five sections are counted for each player.
2. Set combinations are described by the coach according to the standard of the player.

Two Balls

Teams of two. Each player serves at the same time and the object is to keep two balls in play as long as possible. The largest number of strikes is counted for each team within a five minute period.

These games can be played on a number of tables at the same time with winners moving up the hall. This method of circulation is often used for normal match play and ensures that players are thoroughly integrated.

Excess of Players to Tables

Not only can fun games assist in organised sessions for large numbers of players, but improvisation of equipment can also be made to assist. Often I, like many other

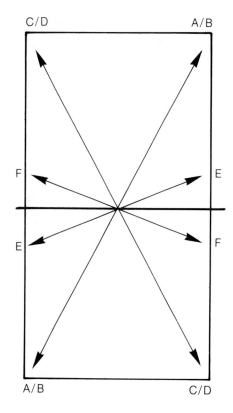

C/D   A/B

F   E

E   F

A/B   C/D

*Fig 104   This method maximises the use
of table space and is quite often
used at rallies and coaching
seminars.*

coaches, have placed four dining tables to create a makeshift table tennis table. Combinations of two tables placed end to end or slightly offset can allow players to practise whilst waiting their turn in the main arena.

One table tennis table can be used to keep a large number of starters occupied, with each pair of players playing down a set line with set strokes (*Fig 104*). If necessary, doubles play can even take place along the diagonals.

Half a table tennis table placed against a good surfaced wall will allow two players to play alternate strokes similar to squash.

All these activities will help to keep the interest of pupils, particularly in early development.

6 Competitive Play

For most people, learning all the basics and putting them to work in practice is only the start. There is, in the human system, a constant need to compare oneself against others, particularly in sport. Table tennis provides ample, if not too much, facility for competitive activities. There is coverage from the early ages at school right through to retiring age.

School

School is often the first place where you can compete with others around you. In many schools there are organised competitions, and in some areas local groups of schools have formed their own schools leagues.

The biggest problem will be to restrict yourself in the amount of competitive play, particularly if there is too little pressure and winning is easy. The local town leagues provide a much stronger background, often with several divisions to cater for varying standards.

Clubs

Most countries have their own Table Tennis Association, with players registered through affiliated clubs. A list of these clubs is available from The International Table Tennis Association.

Joining a good club where there are correct facilities and equipment, as well as the right decorum is the very best advice that you will ever receive. Too many players find themselves in clubs with one table and twenty players, all wishing to practise and compete. Never accept second best. If necessary, form your own club but allow sufficient table time for every member.

Never be afraid of entering tournaments. The competition in some will be far too strong, but you will learn much and gain valuable experience for the next time.

Tournaments

Taking the English Table Tennis Association just as an example, there is a structure that moves through from school to league and then county, regional and national. All levels tend to have intergroup matches and squads from which to pick up their teams. In addition, there are many open tournaments in various parts of the country throughout the season.

At first, when you are trying to gain experience, it is a good idea to enter as many as possible. If and when you are eliminated, check the competition board to find out when matches are scheduled featuring players who have more ability and knowledge than you. Make a study of the match by recording such details as how points were won or lost and the way in which certain players can cope with shots that you find difficult. Look at their footwork and body actions, and in particular watch out for the winning player's positive mental attitude.

As you progress up the ladder there will always be more pressure upon you to play competitive table tennis. Each and every tournament organiser will try to sign you; schools, clubs, leagues and counties will all make their demands. But top players need to practise and to build their game both physically and mentally.

Coaching

Finding yourself a good registered coach can add several points to your game. There are different levels of awards within the coaching structure and as you increase your game quality so you should move to more advanced coaches. Never forget the one you started with though, as he was probably more instrumental in your progress than the others.

Summer Camps

In the off peak times most associations run summer camps for personal performance training. These last for one or two weeks and are supervised by National Coaches. I have attended very many and can safely say that not only do you increase your game capability, but you will find many new friends to make your table tennis into the source of pleasure that it should always be.

TACTICS AGAINST VARIOUS STYLES

It is impossible to categorise every style of play because of the numerous permutations available, but it is worth considering the concepts and the most popular styles.

In the early days of table tennis a player who chopped or backspun the ball was known as a defensive player and the one who topspun or drove the ball was an attacker. Today's players often defend using a topspin lob or slow topspin, whilst playing way back from the base line. Thus, the definition of a defensive player could be: a player who attempts to win points by forcing his opponent into making a mistake. The key factor is consistency. The definition of an attacker would then be: a player who attempts to win the point based on the strength and quality of his own stroke. The key factor being aggression.

To decide which main theme to adopt, you should consider what type of person you are at this stage. If you are a person of exceptional outgoing personality (extrovert), you may be more successful as an attacker. If you are inclined to control your emotions and hate the thought of risk-taking, then perhaps you are more likely to succeed with a game related more to defence or even defence plus counterhitting, rather than all-out attack. Do not assume that because you win points when using a particular style at present, such a style will be best for you in the future. Consult your coach for advice and assessment. Sometimes the physical make-up of your body dictates that you would be better adopting a less agile style of game or vice versa.

At present, there are more attacking players at the top of the world ratings than pure defensive ones, but as players find new ways to combat speed and spin so the game could progress differently. Therefore, what is happening in international play may not be the game for the future. There are strengths and weaknesses within every style, and it is therefore difficult to make hard and fast rules about how to deal with each main style. Thus, you should evaluate each player against whom you play on his merit. However, the following are certain ploys worth considering.

Half-volley Blocker

The blocking style of game requires a player to feed off his opponent's speed and spin. If you hit the ball hard, it is returned fast. If he takes the ball on the half-volley this decreases the time available for you to get ready for the next stroke. It follows that if you have too long a follow-through you will be in difficulty against such a player unless you:

1. Shorten your stroke.
2. Slow down the speed of the ball.
3. Play the ball back to the same spot continuously to stop him switching from your backhand to your forehand.

Blockers love to angle the balls and they can do this best with balls of short length. Therefore, always attempt to play the ball reasonably high to the base line, aiming your own kill to the wings. Some blockers are good at covering the whole of the base line, but are weak against a long driven ball to their crossover point.

Another ploy worth trying is to slow down your hit and increase and vary the amount of spin whilst attempting to disguise it. This will present the blocker with problems in trying to adjust his bat angles correctly and may offer you an opportunity for a kill shot.

If you are a blocker you need to practise switching play from one corner to the other; increase your chances of success by including the odd flick to show your opponent that you can punish any bad length balls.

Combination Bat Player

This is a player who uses a bat on which there are completely contrasting rubbers on either side. There are several variations but the most popular bat is one which has rubber with long pimples facing outwards on one side and reversed rubber on the other.

When they first came out they presented a massive problem, but new rules now stipulate that a bat must have red rubber on one side and black on the other. By watching your opponent's bat, you can see the colour and assess the effect before deciding on

your own counterstroke. This still gives many players the problem of deciphering the effects of the spin being produced at very fast reaction times.

A player using such a bat has to learn and master a complete range of strokes for each rubber. If he uses the art of twiddling (turning the bat over constantly to confuse the opponent) he still has to know how to handle oncoming balls with both his backhand and his forehand. A chopping action using long pimples produces little or no spin, whereas a chop using reverse rubber produces a heavy backspin.

If you wish to adopt this style you must remember that there will be a different angle of bat and a different follow-through for the same stroke played with the different rubbers. In my view, only an already accomplished player should consider changing to this type of bat because it can present as many problems to the player as to the opponent.

When playing against a combination bat player, instead of creating problems for yourself on his returns reduce the amount of spin you apply to the ball and keep your play slow and long. This way he has nothing to feed on. Add an occasional chop to the long pimpled side and his return will be a topspinning ball that you should drive back with aggression. Watch the services very carefully because a chopping action using the long pimples will have no backspin, whereas if he uses the reverse rubber there will be a considerable amount of backspin and quite often sidespin.

Looper

When playing against players who consistently loop the ball it is generally bad practice to use chop because this assists them to increase the spin even more. It is better to play a floating ball (one with little spin) and

Fig 105   Desmond Douglas, the England No. 1 (and a left-handed player), executing a drop shot.

to keep the ball to a short length. Attackers should try to switch the ball from side to side as this makes it difficult for the looper to use full looping strokes, because of the extra length of stroke necessary to produce them. Try playing to the looper's backhand by always serving to his forehand side of the table and then switching. There are players who have a backhand loop, but the majority tend to loop forehand and drive backhand.

When serving, keep the ball short and low and introduce the flicks and blocks with a closed angle bat. It is much more difficult to loop a fast topspin ball, and the degree of accuracy needed to sustain long rallies usually favours the other player.

If you are adopting a looping game it will pay you to practise both looping and smashing sequences, because of the tendency of the looper to overhit what are normally simple high kill shots.

When playing against a chopper, vary the length by playing a short and long game to upset his footwork. Also try looping to each corner with a smash down the centre to his crossover point.

Penholder

I myself played pen grip for the first five years of my career. The pen grip player holds the bat in a similar manner to how you hold a pen. The thumb and forefinger close round the handle near to the blade, whilst the other three fingers support the back of the bat. The three fingers tend to alter their position according to the type of shot being produced. This grip, favoured by Asian players, has some distinct strengths and weaknesses.

Strengths

1. You can disguise where you are going to place the ball until the very last moment by

simple wrist actions.
2. You only use one side of the bat, which gives you faster recovery time.
3. You can hit easily over the table.
4. You can move from forehand to backhand quicker than a shakehands grip.
5. The style tends to assist good movement patterns.
6. There is no crossover point.

Weaknesses (Figs 106 & 107)

1. The penholder requires more agility to get into position.
2. The backhand side can be quite a problem for some players and often looks awkward. Players who have overcome this, however, usually reach very advanced positions in the sport.
3. It can be vulnerable to sidespins.
4. Penholders are at their weakest when driven away from the table and angled.
5. Pen grip takes more controlling, particularly with base line balls.

A penholder needs to adopt a side to square stance along his base line with the right foot slightly behind the left. When making a forehand drive the weight should be transferred from the right foot to the left. After the shot the weight should be transferred back to the right foot ready for the next stroke. The position of a pen grip player should be close to the table for maximum effect.

When playing against a penholder it can be quite fatal to attempt to penetrate the backhand side, because this is normally strong due to the amount of practice it has received from others in the past. The pen grip player has learned to live with it and often either moves round to his forehand quite easily or else produces a cunningly angled return which has you on the defensive. Tactics should include long length balls

Fig 106 *Wide-angled balls to the back-hand can present the pen grip player ...*

Fig 107 *... with difficulties and awkward body actions.*

to his far forehand, with a degree of sidespin to carry the ball even further away. Do not play too many short balls as penholders can be simply devastating at punishing these shots. Try high returns to the backhand when switching from their forehand side.

Left-handers

Left-handers tend to do well at table tennis. I myself am left-handed so have personal experience of the situation. There are many discussions as to why left-handers do well. Some believe that it is because the natural forehand drive of the right-hander is so constantly played to a left-hander's backhand that it becomes very strong, and added to this he still has his own natural forehand making a good two wing player. Others argue that it is because the left-hander is domin-

ated by the right-hand side of the brain, which gives people creativity and intuitive and emotional reactions. Whatever the reason, the left-hander does cause a great deal of upset to the right-hander. Often set pieces previously practised by the right-hander are ineffective. These set pieces take the form of practice patterns where the third or fifth ball is used to create a kill shot to the weakest point. Without some adjustment, they will be played to the natural forehand of the left-hander.

If you are left-handed, you should consider concentrating on a backhand block/flick together with a topspin or forehand loop drive. This will cater for a right-hander's natural forehand to your backhand by returning it with interest.

If playing against a left-hander, try playing the ball to their far forehand position, because they tend to take up their stance nearer to the right-hand side of the table ready to make a switch to their natural forehand. This move will certainly test their footwork and leave you the opportunity of penetrating deep on their backhand court.

Choppers

Although there are many players who just use the chopping action and refuse to hit, waiting instead for their opponent to make a mistake, the game is gradually changing to force even these players to play an occasional counterhit or attacking stroke. Too many choppers can be beaten by the loop stroke, when varied, so that the odd ball is returned high resulting in a kill shot.

If you are a chopper, you can improve your game considerably by adding some form of counterhit or attacking stroke to your skill so that the attacker cannot afford to play any loose or high balls which he might otherwise attempt.

If you are playing against a chopper, do not play regular patterns of play but try to vary the spin, length, timing and speed of your shots so that he never settles into a routine. Choppers generally love to wear down their attackers and once you stop offering all the variations they will invariably win. Of course, initial probing might show you a specific weakness when they change from

their backhand to their forehand but this is not normally sufficient. When serving, a short service will stop them applying much underspin and should therefore be adopted as the main service, intermingled with the occasional long topspin service to the corners.

Spoilers

I define spoilers as players who have unusual or weird strokes. They make these strokes in a completely different way to any conventional methods and do not conform to predetermined guidelines. Often, as players, they can be difficult to beat at local league level, but seldom succeed above this because the better player has searched for and found serious weaknesses which the inexperienced person has failed to find.

If playing against a spoiler, try playing the ball to each wing with long length balls to force him to change constantly from backhand to forehand and to make accurate returns as far from the net as possible.

All Players

In the end, you can only beat a player by keeping the ball in play longer than him. To do this you need to remember that your game should be built on the ability to play *whole skills* rather than just strokes.

7 Setting Goals

MENTAL APPROACH

In order to achieve real success at table tennis you must acknowledge the fact that there will be many times when you will lose a match. For instance, although over 100 people enter a tournament, there is only one winner and the other 99 are losers somewhere along the line.

You must never accept defeat easily, but this should not affect your attitude to the winner and you must always learn to give credit where it is due. To be truly competitive you must conquer the fear of losing and commence every game believing in your ability to win. Players who settle for playing at a level where they produce ninety per cent success are unlikely to be giving themselves the opportunity of progressing beyond their current standard.

There are many players today who have opted out of the fight for the top because they are unable to see that defeat can also create an opportunity for building a better game. My advice to you is to learn from the mistakes of these players, carefully study and always keep in mind the golden rules for success.

Golden Rules for Success

1. Always be striving to improve your play.
2. Never accept anything less than your best performance.
3. Use every defeat as a stepping stone for advancement.
4. Concentrate your mind on the game and not on outside influences.

5. Play the ball and not the reputation of your opponent.

1. Strive to Improve your Play

Remember four key words: test; technique; tactics; and temperament.

Continuously, and as part of your overall plan, *test* yourself against better known players. Never shirk the experience because you may be made to look silly. The knowledge gained can prove immensely valuable to you in your future development programme.

Study your *techniques*. Eliminate any known weaknesses as well as concentrating on your strengths. The saving of points is as valuable as winning points, if not so spectacular. Beware of playing to the crowd.

Study your *tactics*. Stretch your imagination when playing. Watch the opponent's methods and capitalise on them. Constantly review better players and their strategies. Observe the best play available for new ideas.

Temperament – remember the saying ERIC: Emotional Reaction Inhibits Control.

The development of a good temperament demands continuous study of your own attitudes and behaviour.

2. Your Best Peformance

Do not be satisfied with any play that is not stretching you to your full potential. Make no excuses for yourself and never take out your frustrations on others.

3. Defeat as a Stepping Stone

Study every defeat carefully and analyse it using the formula: SWOT.

Strengths What strengths did you have that proved effective? What strengths did your opponent have that won points?

Weaknesses What weaknesses were there in your own game? Were they in ball control, table control or opponent control?

Opportunities What opportunities are there to improve your game quality or tactics the next time you meet.

Threats Did your opponent show up any likely future threats from others that you must take action on?

4. Concentrate your Mind on the Game

Keep your eyes within the confines of the playing area. Focus your attention on your bat or other fixed object, such as the net, and don't allow yourself to be caught in the trap of looking at others, perhaps for advice or ideas. The time spent on these activities could be put to far better use studying your timing point or a likely weakness in your opponent's game.

Concentrate your mind and physical efforts on doing your best with each ball. All too often games are lost by well-meaning supporters trying to coach basics in a competitive situation.

5. Play the Ball

Every champion will be beaten at some time; on many occasions the odds-on favourite has lost. Ignore the name at the other end of the table and instead see only a bat and a faceless body. Forget that it is highly improbable you can win because you are playing say, Desmond Douglas, but devote your entire attention to playing your best shot against each return.

The tendency of lesser players is to compromise and attempt safety play which seldom puts any pressure on the other players allowing them to increase their standards and application.

ANALYSIS OF YOUR GAME

I wonder how many players of great potential never realised their full capability because they were unable to understand what they did well or why they did it well.

Look at *Fig 108*. Everybody has a place somewhere on the wheel. The Unconscious Incompetent is quite often a big fish in a little

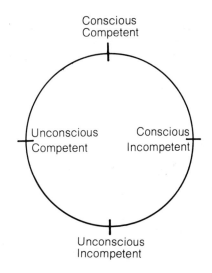

Fig 108   Goal setting.

pond, whilst the Unconscious Competent could be a top player unable to improve. Coaches tend to be drawn from the area between twelve and three o'clock.

Be sure of yourself and your game by having your game analysed by a qualified coach. The method is quite simple and just requires reviewing your game over a short period, for example three different match nights. Recordings are made of such items as:

1. The number and type of unforced errors.
2. The number of service faults.
3. The number of bad service returns and the method used.
4. The number of games lost when leading at the latter stages of a game.
5. The number of bad returns due to inconsistent strokes.
6. Inability to cope with certain rubbers.
7. Mental attitudes when losing at the halfway stage of a game.
8. Poor or no footwork when under pressure.
9. Bad recovery or anticipation.

Sometimes more than one person may be used to record the differing facts. The idea is to build up a complete picture of your game by first breaking it down into small segments and then reconstructing it like a jigsaw puzzle to look for 'causes' rather than effects. Coaches are trained to review the nine points within the basic framework which may well illuminate the true cause. This would then be the subject of your future training sessions.

COACH'S ROLE

In general terms it is the main aim of the coach to bring all of his pupils to their full potential and to keep them there. In order to achieve this a knowledge of sound principles and techniques is essential.

There are various levels of coaching and this is not the book to discuss all the finer details. My advice for anyone interested in coaching is to join in one of the Table Tennis Official Schemes most of which cater for every standard. The teacher at school with four tables and thirty-five pupils can, without a personal high degree of skill, operate very effective and lively sessions following the guidelines of the Teacher's Award. Potential coaches wishing to train in local clubs have many courses and manuals available to help them in teaching the sound principles and organising a series of weekly sessions.

A word of warning: parents do not make the best coaches for their own children. They become so enthusiastic for success that they tend to dominate every move the child makes on and off the table. The parent has a major role in the progress of their family in sport and should be included in all discussions, but there should be a clear understanding of objectives.

For players to enjoy what they are doing, they must have some freedom of choice and eventually in match situations play their own game and not that of a keen but often unconscious incompetent parent who demands attention after each point. Such distraction from whatever source is wrong and is to be discouraged.

Coaches who have players that show signs of poor temperament should continuously work towards some form of control. Remember the acronym ERIC.

I would also like to stress that whilst players should always play within and up to the limit of the rules, the game of table tennis is first and foremost a sport, and sportsmanship and fair play should be ever prevalent even by the most ambitious competitor. Coaches should not have any part in dubious tactics; there are so many that are acceptable and effective without recourse to what I regard as cheating.

Golden Rules for Coaches

Here are ten golden rules which require careful study but will produce greater benefits for all budding international coaches.

1. Coaching should result from an analysis of both the official body and the individual's needs.

Coaches should not be so engrossed with producing a world champion that they forget to consider the views and needs of the player. Unless the player has an internal drive or goal to motivate himself, then it is highly unlikely he will develop to even international standards.
2. Coaching should adopt the right style and method for each session.

Coaches should be flexible in producing programmes and not use the same format regardless of the numbers or standards of players, facilities and time available.
3. Coaching should always be looking for new methods and ways to train and coach.

By moving away from his local area and attending other regional and national coaching functions, the coach will invariably be able to pick up all the latest advances in teaching skills, or alternatively contribute some for others.
4. Coaching should always be based on both opportunity and problem analysis.

When a player's game falls away and there is a problem, the coach should attempt to address the cause. This, if successful, will only bring the player back to normal. The concept of considering what opportunities exist to take the player above the normal should be adopted at all times.
5. Coaching should incorporate good communication skills.

To communicate there has to be a two-way process. Unless the receiver perceives what the speaker has said, there is no communication. The act of telling is not necessarily communicating. Coaches should learn to talk in the same language as the player. Coaching terms should be explained and fully understood. Good coaches will allow their pupils to talk so that they (the coaches) can understand better the needs, difficulties, temperaments and so on of their pupils.
6. Coaching should be integrated and not isolated.

The amount of coaching time available for any player should be broken down and a programme prepared that fully covers the potential requirements of the player for the next season. The use of other coaching centres, specialist coaches, or national courses must be also planned if the programme is to be complete and players allowed to improve with a variety of new partners.
7. Coaching should be supported from the top.

For coaching to achieve its full benefits, there must be support from others involved in the scheme whether it be a club, centre or national function. The idea of paying lip service to coaching will not bring about satisfactory relationships or results.

Parents should opt out from any training or coaching of their children unless they are qualified.
8. Coaching should be ongoing and not a once-off situation.

For any lasting benefit to a player's game, that player requires regular and systematic practice and coaching. The sending of a player to a week's course once a year is not sufficient, although perhaps involves less inconvenience.
9. Coaching should be followed up in a real

life situation.

Table tennis has to be played competitively in some form to create the desire to progress. Players, therefore, should be allowed to compete in matches from an early start. Careful planning of a player's training schedule combined with the right degree of competition will produce the complete player.

10. Coaching should be based on end results.

Whilst class coaching is effective in the early stages and not to be confused with group practice sessions, each player should receive individual coaching based on their abilities and potential plus their willingness to advance.

Coaching is only a means to the end. In the final analysis it is the end results that count.

PROBLEM SOLVING

Many players say they have a problem with their game, but rarely do anything to correct it apart from practising haphazardly. Let us take an example of a player whose game has recently deteriorated; how do we go about defining the problem?

What – what exactly is the problem?

When – when did it occur, has it always been there?

Where – where did it first happen (place), where in the game does it occur?

How – how serious is the extent of the problem?

Draw up a specification and then examine it carefully for any changes from the time the game dropped away. Maybe the player has not renewed the rubber recently or even has worn-out shoes. Perhaps the playing conditions have changed with a new table or different lighting. Also look at details such as whether they have changed their job or what different pressures have been placed on them from outside the sport.

Place all the facts down with dates and then project what possible causes there could be that fit the specification, and produce what could be considered the most possible cause (the M.P.C.). The actions to take can then be either to eliminate the cause (corrective action) or minimise the effect (adaptive action).

8 Doubles Play

The game of doubles often plays an important part in the final result of matches from local league play right up to European and World Championships. In fact, it is normally played towards the end of the match where it assumes the role of the decider in a win, draw or lose situation. Insufficient thought by officials and players alike regarding the best combinations of players can have a disastrous effect, yet seldom do they concentrate their efforts on doubles because of the more prestigious recognition given to singles play.

Picking your Partner

There are so many variations of style and so many successful combinations that have proved the critics wrong, that few would like to advocate any fixed rules for fear of criticism. Regardless of this, there are some good guidelines on which to base your choice.

1. Build a partnership.
2. Beware of a clash of styles.
3. Good singles players don't always make good doubles players.
4. Consider compatibility of partner in terms of rapport and motivation.
5. Examine left- and right-handed combinations.

Build a Partnership

Doubles play depends very much upon the ability of each player to understand their partner's stroke production and movement patterns. Without considerable practice to-gether, it is unlikely that you can progress against well-organised but perhaps less skilful players. Not only should you play regularly together, but you should also be able to discuss technical adjustments to your styles to obtain advantages on court.

Clash of Styles

Certain styles do not blend well together, such as perhaps a defensive chopper and a looper. Even this arrangement, however, has been known to succeed.

The normal pattern is to have combinations such as:

1. Two attackers.
2. Two defenders.
3. One defender and one blocker.
4. One looper and one counterhitter.

Good Singles Players

Beware of the good singles player who takes up too much space with long stroke actions and who moves from very wide bases. He may be unable to move out of your way in sufficient time for you to get a good position. Spectacular hitters may not be able to adjust to the fact that there are now two of you needing to play and build on each other's game.

I have seen very good partnerships where one player acts as the placer of the ball (controlled shot) whilst the other uses speed and spin to win the point. This works even better when partners are capable of reversing this role according to play.

Fig 109 The final of the 1986 Men's Doubles at the English Open
Championships.

Fig 110 With a left- and right-handed combination, the back players
have easy access to their forehand.

Fig 111   Two right-handed Internationals. Note the active footwork.

Compatibility of Partner

Temperament and emotional reaction when not compatible can make two good singles players into very poor partners. You have to look upon your partner as a complete part of the team and not someone who has to be carried. You should be able to enjoy the company of your partner and should be similar in your ultimate aim or goals over a period and not just one match.

Left- and Right-handers

Normally the best doubles pairs are made up of one left-hander and one right-hander. This is because both players can produce powerful forehand attacks without getting in each other's way.

Over the years there have been many world class pairs of left- and right-handers.

This, however, has not prevented combinations of two right- or two left-handed players with good attacks on both wings from achieving top honours.

Options Available

Having decided on a partner the next task is to consider the options available.

1. Service is a key factor in doubles. It should be so executed as to stop the opponent from using any form of kill shot or stroke that you know your partner is weak at returning.

Certain sidespin services can win points direct, but if returned can place your partner in very difficult circumstances forcing an easy return that your opponents will put away. Full knowledge of the effect of heavy spin services is an area on which to concentrate in your practice sessions.

2. Sometimes you or your partner may have to sacrifice a particular shot because of the difficulties encountered by a good return. Understanding the effects of each other's strokes requires patience and planning.

3. Doubles play that depends on defensive strokes alone seldom succeeds in today's climate, especially against good topspin loop drive combinations. The attackers are able to control the play and use the table angles to cause the defensive players severe problems.

4. Pre-match consultation is a 'must' if you wish to succeed. The style and methods used by your immediate opponents require analysis and certain decisions. If, for instance, the situation arises where your partner dislikes taking the return from one of the opponents, it would be better for you to give away service so that you can arrange for him to receive these returns to commence with. This way, should the game go to three, you will finish the final receipt of services.

5. Agreement should be reached that if one of you is on a 'high' and winning points with devastating hits, the other should not try to compete but attempt to make openings by clever placements.

6. Agree any secret signals that might help you to understand what actions are likely to take place by one partner and that will assist any possible returns.

7. During any opponent analysis, try to spot the weaker player or a weaker area of the table. Then plot tactics that will concentrate your strengths on these weaknesses.

8. Plan practice sessions against a complete variety of players and evaluate performance afterwards. Try to increase the angles to force opponents wide or alternatively consider playing the ball directly back to the person who has just struck it towards

you. This means that he will have to get out of the way before his partner can have any chance of a return.

9. Don't allow one or two defeats to discourage the partnership, but persevere and evaluate over a season.

10. Try to borrow a video as this will prove invaluable in sorting out problems.

ORDER OF PLAY

In doubles play, if you win the toss you can decide either to serve or receive first and the losers of the toss can decide on which end they will start, or you can decide at which end you wish to commence, leaving the decision as to which team will serve or receive to the opposition. This situation is the same for singles, but the benefits or disadvantages in doubles can be much more acute. This is because of the variations available in to whom you should serve or from whom you should receive.

If you and your partner elect to serve, you have the right to decide which one of you will commence the first five serves. The opposing pair then have the right to decide who will immediately receive these services. Service changes at every five points, with the receiver then becoming the next server.

In the second game, the opposing pair will serve first and will elect which one of them will start the first five points. At your end, the receiver will be whichever one of you did not receive from the player now serving in the first game. This changes the order of play and presents some possible problem combinations or perhaps advantageous ones.

If there is a third game you will decide who serves first and the opposing pair have to play the same order as for the first game. When the score reaches ten there is an automatic change of ends and at this time the opposing pair can, if they wish, order a change of sequence by making you alter which one of you receives or alternatively by changing their order of receiver. In all cases, regardless of the actual score it is the receivers who alter and not the servers.

These rules are designed to give equal advantage to each pair, but there are some tactics which can give you the edge. If you think that the match is going to be a tough one, it is normally best to give away service in the first game in order to ensure that your weakest player plays against the opposition's strongest player first. This sets the order of service and receive so that at the end of a third or deciding match you will be playing your strongest combination and not your weakest one. Some pairs, however, like to get an immediate advantage and move into a commanding lead in order to demoralise the opponents. This means they might either serve or play their strongest player first. Whatever choice you make, I recommend that you consider the possible alternatives and make a decision rather than let fate decide. Even if you lose the right to serve, you can decide to play the first game at the worst end if there is a worst end. This means that in the second game you will be at the best end, and if there is a deciding game you will be at the worst end up to the score of ten, when you again take the best end for the final assault.

If your partner has any known weaknesses of either his backhand or forehand side, these can sometimes be overcome by clever positional play by ensuring that the line of play open to your opposition brings the ball back to your partner's strongest side. Wide angled balls off the sidelines played with just a fast push can get the opposition in a tangle, particularly if they tend to adopt individual receive positions similar to when they play singles rather than a team orien-

tated ready position.

MOVEMENT PATTERNS

If you are a left- and right-handed combination with good forehands, then the best pattern to adopt is for the left-hander to come into the receive position from the right-hand side of the table and to retreat in the same direction. This places both players with their forehands commanding more of the table area.

If you are both right-handers or both left-handers it may be better for you to move in and out from the side where you are standing at the start of each service sequence. It would be wise to develop a strong backhand service in order not to take up too much table room and thus block your partner from taking returns made to the right-hand court. Of

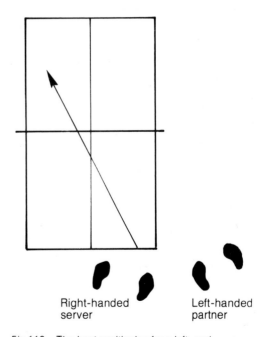

Right-handed server   Left-handed partner

Fig 112   The best positioning for a left- and right-handed combination.

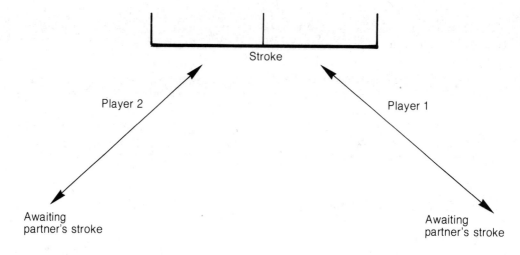

Stroke

Player 2

Player 1

Awaiting
partner's stroke

Awaiting
partner's stroke

Fig 113   Two right-handed players moving in and out along diagonals.

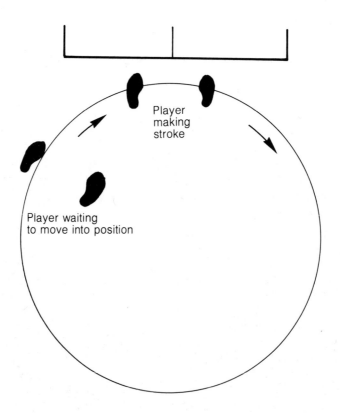

Player
making
stroke

Player waiting
to move into position

*Fig 114   Circling action footwork: the players move clockwise round
each other.*

course, in all cases, there are times when you will be playing out of position and it is because of this that a complete understanding of your partner's game is essential to determine the best method of allowing access to the varying lines of play for the next striker.

Many players with good backhand flicks may prefer alternative footwork patterns such as creating a circling action. In this the players move around each other in turn in a clockwise direction. Like all other patterns, this will break down at times and it is in these situations where teamwork and co-ordination are of prime importance. Good readers of possible new lines of play can automatically take up a correct position in advance; players with this ability may well be better for the partnership than perhaps a player who has a superior singles record.

MIXED DOUBLES

In mixed doubles, the woman is normally the weaker player and it is the task of the man to shield his partner from the ferocity of the opposing male's strokes by playing in such a way and placing such pressure on that player that he is only able to produce a safety shot.

Woman's Role

A good role for the woman player is to place the ball into difficult positions with varied timing and block shots in order to upset the rhythm of the opposition. She should be capable of serving a short low service of such quality as to prevent any major attack, and produce as an alternative the occasional fast long length topspin service.

Fig 115 Mixed doubles involves different playing tactics.

Fig 116   When it is a combination of two right-handers, the waiting
player is often forced away to give room for the partner to play
forehand.

Receive of service can be a big problem to the woman when she is receiving from the man. Therefore, rather than use a defensive or underspun stroke, it is imperative that she practises to develop a good half-volley block or topspin return to counter any opportunity for aggressive play from the opposing pair.

Man's Role

The man must accept responsibility for attacking wherever possible. He should not confuse his partner with too much sidespin as this can sometimes be returned and cause her impossible problems. He may need to encourage his partner when dealing with an awkward sequence and not show anger when or if she misses what he considers to be simple returns. Too often I have seen potentially good partnerships break up because of emotional problems rather than physical skills.

CONCLUSION

Doubles play can be very interesting whilst providing players with excellent opportunities to increase their own personal game. The degree of movement required will help the player with poor footwork, and the playing of strokes whilst on the move (through necessity), can be invaluable for all. If you are a player who needs practice at transferring weight to the forward foot, then doubles play can provide that platform.

In clubs with few tables and many players, the game of doubles offers everyone a chance of practice and competition. The older player too can be extremely effective because of his experience and, when teamed up with a younger player, often acts as a calming influence particularly in critical situations.

9 Equipment

TABLE *(Fig 117)*

The following are some rules, as laid down by the International Table Tennis Federation, in respect of the table.

1. The upper surface of the table, termed the 'playing surface' shall be rectangular, 2.74m (9 feet) long and 1.525m (5 feet) wide, and shall lie in a horizontal plane 760mm (2½ feet) above the floor.
2. The playing surface shall be made of any material and shall yield a uniform bounce of 220-250mm (9 – 10 inches) when a standard ball, preferably of medium bounce, is dropped from a height of 305 mm (12 inches) above it.
3. The playing surface shall be dark coloured, preferably dark green, and matt, with a white line 20mm (¾ inch) wide along each edge.
4. The lines along the 1.525m (5 feet) edges shall be termed 'end lines'.
5. The lines along the 2.74m (9 feet) edges shall be termed 'side lines'.
6. For doubles, the playing surface shall be divided into halves by a white line 3mm wide, running parallel with the side lines, termed the centre line; permanent marking of the centre line on the playing surface shall not invalidate the table for singles play.
7. The playing surface shall be considered to include the top edges of the table, but not the sides of the table top below the edges.

Comment

Although no mention is made in the rules, the table thickness of a wooden playing surface (top) should be 22mm, or as close to that as possible. It normally follows that the thinner the surface, the poorer the quality.

A ball bouncing over a poor quality table leg tends to have a different bounce to a ball bouncing in the middle of the surface. Sometimes the ball does not reach the minimum height required in the rules.

Care of the Table

One inch nominal plywood table tennis tables can be found in many old storage places in old halls or stacked away under stairs and so on. These should not be discarded as rubbish but looked at carefully, because when they are sent back to a main manufacturer (such as John Jacques & Sons) they can be completely refurbished as new, and play with the most excellent quality.

Chips and knocks on the edges of a table tennis table can be filled using 'Brumer stopping', which can later be sanded down to a very smooth finish before reapplying the white line.

Undercarriages sometimes need attention where hinges have broken or new pins are required. Five minutes spent rectifying this makes a firmer and better table.

Surfaces of tables left standing for any length of time should either be covered or kept dust free. A dry or damp cloth can be used, but in no circumstances should deter-

Equipment

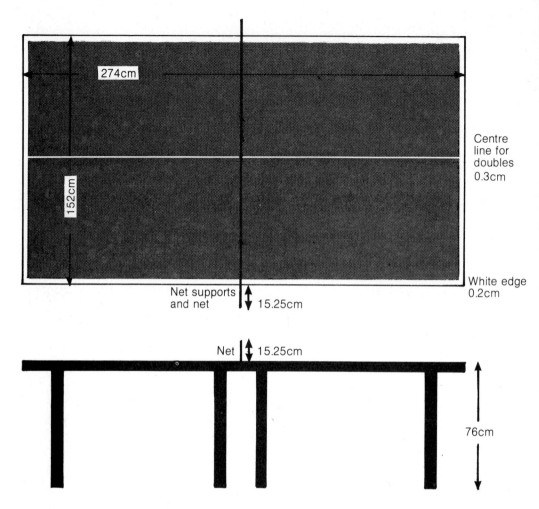

Fig 117   The table tennis table.

gent or polish be applied. A shiny table can be a player's worst enemy.

Storage *(Fig 118)*

If tables are to be taken down for storage or for space utilisation they should always be stacked as follows:

1. On the centre edges.

2. Surface to surface of each section, touching from top to bottom.
3. As near as possible to vertical.

This will help to keep the table from damage to its playing edges and stop warping of top surfaces. If a table is to be used for anything other than table tennis it should be covered with a waterproof covering. In fact, any such idea should be discouraged if at all possible.

Fig 118   *The correct method of table storage can preserve a table in good condition for many years.*

NET

Rules

1. The playing surface shall be divided into two 'courts' of equal size by a vertical net running parallel with the end lines.
2. The net shall be supported by a cord attached at each end to an upright post 152.5mm (6 inches) high. The outside limits for the post being 152.5mm outside the side line.
3. The net, with its suspension, shall be 152.5mm above the playing surface; the bottom of the net, along its whole length, shall be close to the playing surface and the ends of the net shall be close to the supporting posts.

Comment

Always keep a good quality net available for matches and place it in responsible hands or a locked cupboard when not in use. Many places in which I have played are unable to produce a net which conforms to the rules. Many are torn or have been mistreated by others.

Check the height before every match, as a slight error in height can make a great deal of difference in play. It is perhaps better to practise with a net that is slightly higher than the rules rather than one which is lower.

OTHER EQUIPMENT

Ball

If you wish to play table tennis correctly then, in my opinion, the ball must be of three-star brand. Keep stocks in a cool place away from sunlight.

If you suspect the ball is cracked, first smell it if it is celluloid. If you are unable to detect any chemical smell, roll it gently with the bat on the table surface, any cracks should then become apparent. Do not hoard cracked balls in your kit as this may lead you to believe you have a stock on an important occasion when you haven't.

To check whether a ball is completely round try spinning it on the table surface. If there is a defect, the ball will tend to gyrate eccentrically.

For school play use plastic balls and for tournament play use celluloid balls.

Bat

Weight

Bats come in varying shapes, sizes and weights and with varying degrees of speed, spin and control. One should choose a bat which is comfortable in the hand and with as much weight as you think you can manage.

Equipment

A popular myth in table tennis is that you need a super light bat. A bat with greater weight offers greater control over spin and speed, as the speed of ball or weight of ball (spin) has less chance of distorting the angle of the bat on contact. The bat for young players, however, should not be heavier than 156 g (5½ oz).

Blade (Fig 119)

For beginners I advocate the use of a wooden blade of five ply construction. This will allow all-round play and better control. As you improve there are many choices of blades, from a single ply to seven ply.

Some manufacturers have combined different types of wood in the various layers for special effects. The use of a carbon layer mixed amongst the 'plys'. increases the strength and reduces weight, but all these characteristics have to be weighed against the type of rubber applied to the surface.

Bats can be an expensive item. My advice is for you to try out different combinations, borrowing bats from your friends before spending a lot of money only to find you don't like the 'feel'.

The shape of the blade can vary too, with square shapes and oval designs. Each has its merits.

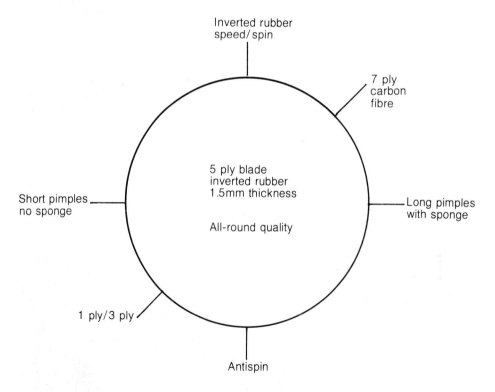

Fig 119   Each line represents a range of graduated attributes associated with certain types of rubbers and blades. In general the area between 6 o'clock and 9 o'clock provides slower effects on the ball.

Fig 120   A few of the different shapes of handles and blades available.
            If necessary, modify the shape where the handle meets the
            blade to make it fit your own hand with maximum comfort.

Fig 121   The bat on the left has medium pimples outward, whilst the bat
            on the right has inverted pimples. Both have a 2.5mm layer of
            sponge.

Centre of Gravity

The position of the centre of gravity, whether it be towards the handle (low) or towards the top edge (high), can assist different styles of play. For instance: if you are a player who likes to switch from forehand to backhand, a low centre of gravity can be a great help; whilst if you prefer to take the ball early and over the table or prefer defensive tactics, then the high centre of gravity will pay dividends. It is a good idea to keep a similar spare bat in your kit in case of breakage.

Rubber *(Fig 121)*

Rubber is produced basically in two forms:

1. Inverted (smooth surface; pimples in – with sponge layer).
2. Pimples out (long or short pimples – with or without sponge layer).

By far the most popular rubber throughout the world is the inverted rubber with sponge layer that has a bias towards speed and spin. The pimpled variety and anti-spin inverted rubbers fall into the highly specialised range that would not be suitable for the majority of the playing population.

Inverted rubber is judged in two ways:

1. By its rebound quality (speed).
2. By its grip quality (spin).

Obviously, the greater the two elements, the more speed and spin. However, for rubber to operate to its full potential it is essential that it is kept scrupulously clean.

Care of Bats and Rubbers

Always keep your bat in a cover as the oxygen in the atmosphere tends to harden the surface and affect the spin characteristics.

Never leave a bat in strong sunlight, as this also makes the surface hard and glossy. Beware of buying bats which have been used for display in sports shop windows. Never store your equipment and bats near to high temperatures such as radiators or chimneys; the rubber will soon be adversely affected.

Resist the use of solvents or abrasives on your rubbers. They will act in the short term, but will increase the speed of deterioration. Wipe rubbers clean of dust with a little water and dry off with light pressure of a dry lint-free rag.

Hands tend to give off an alkali when perspiring and this can often be transferred to the rubber surface. A few drops of household vinegar (very weak acid) will remove this alkali and also grease marks. Wipe afterwards with a damp cloth dipped in water and dry off with a rag.

Watch for edges lifting and seal back down with a rubber glue.

Replacing Rubbers

Duration of Rubbers

Table tennis rubbers are made using a variety of natural and synthetic products. They are often produced in two layers with the top surface developed for high friction efficiency and the lower part for good elasticity. These qualities do have a limited lifespan, so rubber needs to be changed at regular intervals. For the average player I would recommend changing the rubber at the commencement of the season and once again half-way through the season. Players playing at the top level of local associations should aim to change even more frequently.

Method of Replacing

Old rubbers should always be taken off the bat from the side. In instances where the sponge begins to pull away from the wood, heat the rubber slightly or apply a small amount of glue remover or acetone. Rubbers and sponge should be taken off together.

Clean the surface of the bat with a fine glass paper (00) to remove old glue. Smooth on a fine layer of glue (pressure sensitive rubber adhesive) Bostic 1180 (England) or Bostic 299 (New Zealand). Fold the new rubber onto the blade starting from the handle. Turn over and cut with a very sharp knife or scalpel, taking care not to tear the rubber or sponge. Repeat with other side.

FACILITIES

Lighting

All forms of lighting are used today in table tennis centres or sports halls. Although I still prefer the ordinary tungsten bulb arrangement which is specially erected over the table, the use of quartz halogen from a high ceiling does give the player better illumination than, for instance, fluorescent tubes. My main concern is that if halogen lamps are placed over the centre of the table, defensive players are at a disadvantage because they will see a white ball that is approaching them suddenly turn dark, as a shadow is cast because of the lack of back lighting.

Some clubs have clever systems which allow lights suspended over two adjoining tables to be brought together to form a super bank for special matches. This is often done by having five lights with shades connected spaced along a strong wooden pole. This, in turn, is suspended from the ceiling on runners. Two sets of these can be pulled into position or out again very quickly.

Whatever the source of lighting, do keep bulbs and covers, if any, clean and free from dust. Replace duds immediately and have spare bulbs available for others to make emergency changes.

General

It is not easy to dictate where you can play table tennis, but wherever you play something can be done to make it easier for yourself.

The use of large mesh nets between tables and good surrounds at the ends of tables will cut down that painful experience of losing a ball during a crucial part of an important match.

All loose equipment, such as towels and track suits, should be away from the table and not placed under the carriage. I have seen a person break a leg by sliding on a loose garment. The floor should be polish-free and preferably wooden. Certain composite floors play well, but carpeting of any description is wrong and to be strongly discouraged.

Walls and windows often present problems which might be overcome with the use of drapes of a dark material so that the ball will show up in contrast. Sunlight should be excluded by blinds, and draughts by screens as air movement can cause havoc to a ball in flight. (I have had a lot of fun playing in the open in summer on slate tables, when you have to allow for wind direction.)

DRESS

Table tennis can be a very strenuous game regardless of standards, and my advice to all players is to dress correctly for the sport. The guidelines for dress are very simple.

Shirts

These should be of a dark colour and large enough to allow plenty of movement without restriction. Always carry a spare shirt so that if you perspire heavily in one match, you may appear later feeling fresh.

Skirts/Shorts

Again, these should be of a dark coloured material. In the case of shorts make sure that the legs are designed so that they give when you need to take long strides. Larger people can cut a 'V' shape at the bottom of the sides about an inch (2.5 cm) long. This will assist movement considerably.

Track Suits

It is strongly recommended that you have a track suit to keep you warm when not actually playing, but you should not wear it after the initial knock-up unless it is a bitterly cold hall. Matches should always be played so that complete freedom of movement is obtained without any drag resistance. This conserves energy in the physical sense and makes you feel better mentally.

Shoes

Clean, well looked after plimsolls are essential. They should be lightweight yet built for comfort as they can be worn for long periods.

Today there are many designs of sports footwear. Look first at the table tennis manufacturers' catalogues. There you will find many styles developed specially for the speed of turn and grip necessary to play well. Some are made to allow the feet to 'breathe' and keep cool whilst others are said to minimise energy losses by having arcs and ellipses especially fitted.

New sports shoes need breaking in and you should carry this out in practice matches rather than important fixtures.

Socks

White socks are a 'must' to complete the appearance. Beware of wearing ones which are tight around the leg and ankle, as uncomfortable socks can irritate and affect your mental attitude in moments of extreme pressure. Choose those with cushioned soles to help absorb the constant shocks and also to provide more comfort over long periods.

Towel

A good quality towel with a soft absorbent pile should be a standard in everyone's kit.

Kitbag

Regularly sort out your kitbag and throw away all unnecessary items. Check that you have included such items as:

1. Playing bat plus spare identical bat in covers.
2. Rag for cleaning.
3. Supply of three-star balls.
4. Towel.
5. First aid kit – liniment, plasters and aspirins.
6. Net measure.
7. Results pad.
8. Laws of table tennis.
9. A pen and a coin (for when you might have to umpire).
10. A table tennis diary.
11. League or appropriate handbook.
12. Glucose drink or tablets.

Additional items for coaches should include:

13. Chalk and string to make centre lines for doubles.
14. A variety of bats.
15. Coaching manual.
16. Tournament entry forms.
17. Bat repair and rubber replacement kit.
18. Duster (for table cleaning).
19. Skills Award Tests and method of assessment.

20. Spare net and supports.

Of course, not all these items need to be in your immediate kitbag, but it is a good idea to have them available in your car or transport. Some coaches even carry such items as spare bulbs, and screwdrivers to make instant repairs to table legs and undercarriages.

10 Dunlop Skills Award Scheme

Rules for Grade One

Test 1: Objective – to improve 'feel' of bat and ball.
(No table needed for this test.) Demonstrate forehand tap bounce.
Pass: Ten bounces with maximum one error (three attempts allowed).

Test 2: Objective – as Test 1.
As Test 1, played with backhand.

Test 3: Objective – to improve stance and alertness.
(Any table can be used for this test.) Demonstrate a good 'ready' position; slightly crouched, knees slightly bent. Feet apart, more than shoulder width. Bat held lightly, pointing at and ready to track an imaginary oncoming ball.

Test 4: Objective – to improve skill in guiding (not 'hitting') the ball.
Candidate drops ball from 10 inches (25 cm) height at position B and steers it backhand to BT. Controller catches and returns the ball.
Pass: Ten balls with maximum two errors (three attempts allowed).

Test 5: Objective – as Test 4.
Exactly as Test 4 but dropping the ball at position F and steering it forehand to FT.

Test 6: Objective – to improve mobility.
(Again any table of suitable width can be used for this test.)

Demonstrate six movements to either side, F to B, with bat but without ball.
Pass: Use of small skip-steps, moving on toes and never closing feet together.

Test 7: Objective – to improve understanding of position.
Demonstrate ability to steer balls alternately, backhand B to BT and forehand F to FT.
Procedure: Candidate drops ball to bounce net-high at B and steers smoothly backhand to BT. Candidate then moves to F and catches ball thrown there by controller. Candidate then drops ball at F and steers it forehand to FT, moves back to B to catch ball thrown by controller, and so on. Test continues until twenty alternate steering actions have been played.
Pass: Twenty alternate steering actions with no more than five errors.

Test 8: Objective – to encourage the idea of partnership in learning.
Pass: Candidate must act as controller (e.g. catcher and thrower) to another Grade One candidate. Assessor to judge co-operation and team spirit etc.

Note

Throughout tests for Grades One and Two the following abbreviations will be used to denote specific areas on the table *(Fig 122)*:

B – Backhand contact area.

F – Forehand contact area.
BT – Backhand target area.
FT – Forehand target area.

A sheet of A3 paper (or two pieces of A4) is ideal for indicating the size of target area and can be moved to suit the test.

Rules for Grade Two

Test 1: Objective – to practise 'receive' of mini-service.
Note: Always make it clear that the mini-serve is a slow, short practice ball to improve touch and placing and is not a correct match service. (Contact only with opponent's side of table.)
Procedure: Backhand return from B to BT against controller's mini-serve BT to B.
Pass: Four out of five balls, correctly returned to controller, and not beyond area BT (three attempts allowed).

Test 2: Objective – as Test 1.
Procedure: Forehand returns (F to FT) of controller's mini-serves (F to FT).
Pass: As Test 1.

Test 3: Objective – the practice of 'good returns'.
Procedure: Play ten successive continuous slow speed returns with forehand from half-court F to half-court FT and half-court BT alternately. Controller or approved partner must return, slow speed, all balls to F.
Pass: Maximum one error (three attempts allowed). An error by a controller does not count against the candidate, who can continue his score.

Test 4: Objective – as Test 3.
Procedure: Play with backhand from half-court B to half-court BT and FT alternately.
Pass: As Test 3.

Test 5: Objective – similar to Test 3.
Procedure: Candidate must make sixteen slow speed returns, alternating forehand with backhand.
Pass: Maximum two errors.
(Controller should not put candidate under pressure.)

Test 6: Objective – to assess candidate's table tennis knowledge.
Answer questions about:

1. A correct table.
2. A correct net.
3. A correct bat.
4. Procedures in case of a net-ball.
5. Regulations about clothing.

Note

As the Grade Two Award deals with developing rally skills, a steady controller is needed; this may be the assessor, or a more experienced junior under supervision.

Rules for Grade Three

Test 1: All backhand push control (from two points, returning to one target).
Using sound footwork for training, return thirty slow push shots (which have been placed, slowly, by controller from C1, alternately, to areas B and M). Candidate to use only backhand push strokes, all played back to area C1 *(Fig 123)*.
Pass: Thirty successes before fourth error.

Test 2: All forehand controlled topspin drive.
Against steady returns from controller, play thirty forehand drive strokes, maintaining direction on one diagonal only, without increasing speed.
Pass: Thirty successes before fourth error.

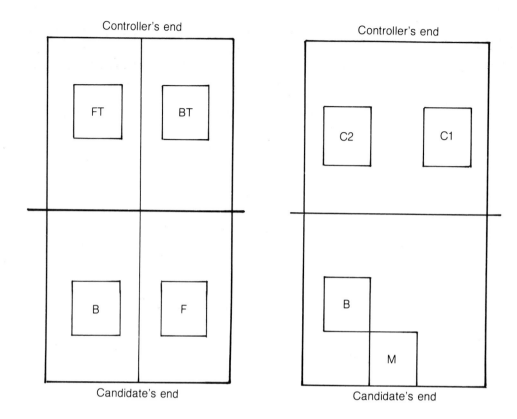

Controller's end

FT   BT

B   F

Candidate's end

Fig 122   Grades One and Two.

Controller's end

C2   C1

B

M

Candidate's end

Fig 123   Grade Three.

Test 3: Combined control.
Return thirty slow balls from controller by playing, in strict alternation, backhand push and forehand drive.
Note: Controller should feed balls alternately to B and M.
Pass: Thirty successes before fourth error.

Test 4: Backhand 'block' returns.
Against medium speed topspin from controller, return ball by simple rebound technique, i.e. straight-line 'reflection', from the peak of bounce position. Maintain direction on one diagonal.
Pass: Thirty successes before fourth error.

Test 5: Short touch services.
1. From correct position behind the base line serve short forehand services so as to clear the net and bounce twice on the table.
2. As above but service with backhand.
Pass: In each case, five successes to be achieved within eight attempts.

Test 6: Long topspin services.
1. From correct position serve with forehand, ball to land beyond target area C2.
2. As above but service with backhand, ball to land beyond target area C1.
Pass: In each case, five successes within eight attempts.

Rules for Matchplayer Level

Test 1: Return of varied services.
Required: Suitable push or attack services delivered with medium strength sidespins, including elements of topspin and chop.
Pass: Sixteen successes before fifth error.

Test 2: Services variation.
Deliver services of varying strength, incorporating sidespin, alternating left and right.
Pass: Sixteen successes before fifth error.

Test 3: Combining drive and push – forehand.
Return thirty balls, which have been alternately pushed and chopped, by using (respectively) topspin drive and short push shots, played alternately, forehand, on one diagonal line. Topspin and backspin must be clearly displayed in the rallies.
Pass: Thirty correct before fifth error.

Test 4: Combining drive and push – backhand.
As Test 3 but using backhand throughout.
Pass: As Test 3.

Test 5: Combining (chopped) defensive returns with push – forehand.
Return thirty balls which have been alternately driven and pushed, on same line, by using, respectively, backspin defensive returns and short pushes, played alternately on same line, all forehand. Topspin and backspin must be clearly displayed in the rallies.
Pass: As Test 3.

Test 6: Combining (chopped) defensive returns with push – backhand.
As Test 5 but using backhand throughout.
Pass: As Test 3.

Test 7: Maintaining attack against topspin from controller.
Maintain ten triple sequences thus: two forehand topspin drives plus one backhand block.
Pass: Ten good sequences before fifth error.

Test 8: As Test 7 but
Sequences of two backhand drives plus one forehand block.
Pass: Ten good sequences before fifth error.

Test 9: Laws and rules.
Answer ten 'everyday' questions on laws and match procedure. Points allowed: three

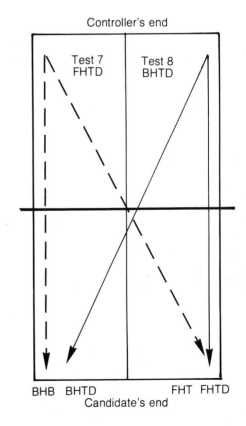

Fig 124   Matchplayer level.

for a complete answer; two for correct 'sense'; one for a part answer.
Pass: Score twenty-two out of thirty.

Note

1. This level can only be assessed by ETTA Club or Diploma Coaches.
2. Candidates must already have passed the Grade Three Award.
3. The assessor must satisfy himself that the quality of the candidate's stroke work is satisfactory.
4. Before scoring each test the assessor must witness and approve a 'dry land' demonstration of the ensuing stroke action(s).
5. Throughout the test the following abbreviations will be used:

FHTD – Forehand topspin drive.
BHTD – Backhand topspin drive.
FHB – Forehand block.
BHB – Backhand block.

Rules for Masters Level

Test 1: Topspin driving under pressure, forehand and backhand.
Play thirty alternate topspin drives to one point, against half-volley returns which have been placed alternately to areas F and B. Good position and footwork required throughout.
Pass: Thirty correct before third error.

Test 2: Counter-driving, close and distant, forehand.
Return thirty counter-drives by means of forehand counter-drives in sequences of two thus: two 'close', two 'distant', two 'close' etc. All returns kept on the same diagonal.
Pass: Third error fails.

Test 3: Counter-driving, close and distant, backhand.
As Test 2 but using backhand counter-drive.
Pass: Third error fails.

Test 4: Combining forehand and backhand topspin drives.
Against slow chopped returns, which have been placed alternately to areas J and K, by playing twenty forehand and backhand topspin drives, alternately directed diagonally to areas H and G.
Pass: Third error fails.

Test 5: Combining forehand and backhand defensive backspin returns.
Return twenty drives, received alternately on corner areas J and K by means of, respectively, forehand and backhand chopped returns, to area L.
Pass: Third error fails.

Test 6: Sequences of topspin and backspin strokes.
Play fifteen double sequences of forehand chop and backhand drive against balls which have been respectively driven to the forehand and pushed to the backhand, and returned to area G.
Pass: Fourth error fails.

Test 7: Sequences of topspin and backspin strokes.
Play the reverse of Test 6, i.e. backhand for forehand and vice versa. Return to area H.
Pass: Fourth error fails.

Test 8: Backhand attack distribution.
Play ten triple sequences thus: dropshot to area E; backhand drive to area H; backhand drive to area G; and repeat etc. Controller returns all balls to area M with backspin. Candidate may keep ball in play with simple placing shots between the actual scoring

sequences.
Pass: Fourth error fails.

Test 9: Display understanding of loop-topspin forehand.
Play eight double sequences thus: '9 o'clock loop' against chopped return followed by '12 o'clock loop' against blocked return. Sequence must be according to opportunity, a continuous rally is not demanded.
Pass: Third error fails.

Test 10: Triple sequences.
Play ten triple sequences of backhand top-spin drive, forehand loop and forehand drive to area L, from balls which have been blocked by the controller to areas J, F and J respectively.
Pass: Fourth error fails.

Test 11: Third ball attack.
Deliver ten backhand services of varying lengths and spin which are to be flicked or pushed alternately to K and J. The candidate must follow up with a suitable third ball attack.
Pass: Fourth error fails.

Test 12: As Test 11 but forehand serves.
Pass: Fourth error fails.

General Notes Regarding Assessment

1. Candidates should be allowed time to warm up.
2. An assessor should not apply 'engineer's standards' to suggested targets. Allowance can be made for meritorious effort and obvious short-term improvement potential.
3. Assessors should appoint suitable controllers to give each candidate a fair chance

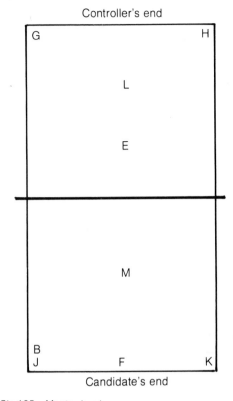

Fig 125 *Master level.*

and a scorer to keep count of successes and errors.
4. Controllers should be able to place a steady ball to required targets at the right pace. Any mistakes by the controller, unlucky balls or balls which are not appropriate to a particular test should be called as 'let'. Candidate should restart from existing score.
5. Assessors will be as follows:
Grades One and Two: teachers, club leaders, league officials, ETTA students and coaches.
Grade Three: holders of ETTA Teaching Certificate or higher. Additionally, experienced teachers and club leaders etc. may apply to the organiser for approval as a Grade Three Assessor.

USE OF EQUIPMENT AND SPACE

Many coaches working in school or club situations often face a lack of facilities which may appear to limit opportunities. Here are a few ways in which you can optimise the use of equipment and space.

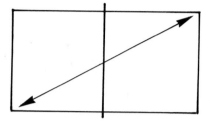

Two players may use the long channel for pushing, driving chopping ...

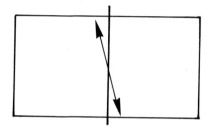

... or the short channel for backhand, forehand or alternate backhand/forehand touch play.

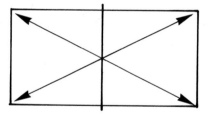

Four players may use the long channels for counter driving, pushing, blocking ...

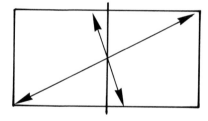

... or the short channel for touch play and the long channel for driving and looping.

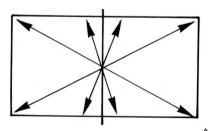

Eight players may use short and long channels for touch play practice ...

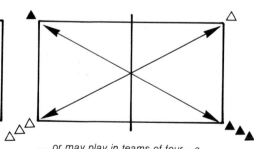

... or may play in teams of four – a controller feeding to three other players.

104

School PE benches, with a small cardboard 'net', are ideal for practising backhand push strokes.

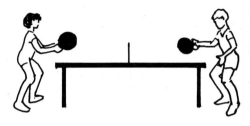

Plastic-topped school tables are ideal for touch play practices.

The hall or gymnasium could be set out for practice with three table tennis tables and other apparatus to incorporate sixteen players who move around this 'circus'.

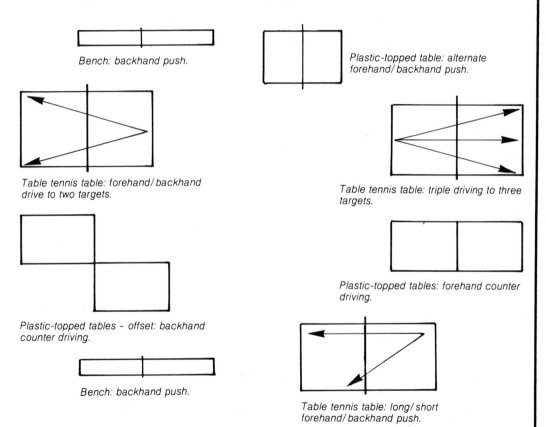

Bench: backhand push.

Plastic-topped table: alternate forehand/backhand push.

Table tennis table: forehand/backhand drive to two targets.

Table tennis table: triple driving to three targets.

Plastic-topped tables – offset: backhand counter driving.

Plastic-topped tables: forehand counter driving.

Bench: backhand push.

Table tennis table: long/short forehand/backhand push.

Each pair of players moves around the circus spending four minutes on each exercise – they change partners and repeat the exercise.

Dunlop Skills Award Scheme

Matchplayer: ETTA Club or Diploma Coaches.

Dunlop Master: ETTA Diploma Coaches only.

6. A candidate may start at Grade Two on the recommendation of a teacher or club leader. Similarly Grade Three, if the assessor knows that the candidate already has a fair practice standard.

7. Grades One and Two may be assessed on the same occasion provided the assessor is satisfied as to the candidate's all-round practical experience.

8. A Diploma Coach assessing a Dunlop Masters Award candidate may take into account known match results but should not pass the candidate unless an acceptance of training disciplines is also apparent.

9. After completing a test successful candidates should be asked for their full names. The assessor should collect these together with £1 for the badge and certificate fees. When a minimum of five names have been collected by the assessor they should be sent, together with covering letter, to the Awards Organiser at the ETTA. The appropriate badges and certificates will then be returned to the assessor in due course. The assessor should add his signature to those already on the certificate before presenting it to the Award Winner.

Laws of the Game

THE LAWS OF TABLE TENNIS

(See also Regulations for International Competitions)

3.1 The Table

3.1.1 The upper surface of the table, known as the 'playing surface', shall be rectangular, 2.74m long and 1.525m wide, and shall lie in a horizontal plane 76cm above the floor.

3.1.2 The playing surface shall include the top edges of the table but not the sides of the table top below the edges.

3.1.3 The playing surface may be of any material and shall yield a uniform bounce of about 23cm when a standard ball is dropped on to it from a height of 30cm.

3.1.4 The playing surface shall be uniformly dark coloured and matt, with a white line 2cm wide along each edge.

3.1.4.1 The lines along the 2.74m edges shall be known as 'side lines'.

3.1.4.2 The lines along the 1.525m edges shall be known as 'end lines'.

3.1.5 The playing surface shall be divided into two equal 'courts' by a vertical net running parallel with the end lines, and shall be continuous over the whole area of each court.

3.1.6 For doubles,

3.1.6.1 each court shall be divided into two equal 'half courts' by a white line 3mm wide, known as the 'centre line', running parallel with the side lines;

3.1.6.2 the centre line shall be regarded as part of the server's right half court and of the receiver's right half court.

3.2 The Net Assembly

3.2.1 The net assembly shall consist of the net, its suspension and the supporting posts.

3.2.2 The net shall be suspended by a cord attached at each end to an upright post 15.25cm high, the outside limits of the post being 15.25cm outside the side line.

3.2.3 The top of the net, along its whole length, shall be 15.25cm above the playing surface.

3.2.4 The bottom of the net, along its whole length, shall be as close as possible to the playing surface and the ends of the net shall be as close as possible to the supporting posts.

3.3 The Ball

3.3.1 The ball shall be spherical, with a diameter of 38mm.

3.3.2 The ball shall weigh 2.5g.

3.3.3 The ball shall be made of celluloid or similar plastics material and shall be white or yellow, and matt.

3.4 The Racket

3.4.1 The racket may be of any size, shape or weight but the blade shall be flat and rigid and shall be made of wood.

3.4.1.1 At least 85 per cent of the blade by thickness shall be of natural wood.

3.4.1.2 An adhesive layer within the blade may be reinforced with fibrous material such as carbon fibre, glass fibre or compressed paper, but shall not be thicker than 7.5 per cent of the total thickness or 0.35mm, whichever is smaller.

3.4.2 A side of the blade used for striking the ball shall be covered with either ordinary pimpled rubber with pimples outwards having a total thickness including adhesive of not more than 2mm, or sandwich rubber with pimples inwards or outwards having a total thickness including adhesive of not more than 4mm.

3.4.2.1 'Ordinary pimpled rubber' is a single layer of non-cellular rubber, natural or synthetic, with pimples evenly distributed over its surface at a density of not less than 10/sq cm and not more than 50/sq cm.

3.4.2.2 'Sandwich rubber' is a single layer of cellular rubber covered with a single outer layer of ordinary pimpled rubber, the thickness of the pimpled rubber not being more than 2mm.

3.4.3 The covering material shall extend up to but not beyond the limits of the blade, except that the part nearest the handle and gripped by the fingers may be left uncovered or covered with any material and may be considered part of the handle.

3.4.4 The blade, any layer within the blade and any layer of covering material or adhesive shall be continuous and of even thickness.

3.4.5 The surface of the covering material on a side of the blade, or of a side of the blade if it is left uncovered, shall be uniformly dark coloured and matt; any trimming round the edge of the blade shall be matt and no part of it shall be white.

3.4.6 Slight deviations from continuity of surface or uniformity of colour due to accidental damage, wear or fading may be allowed provided that they do not significantly change the characteristics of the surface.

3.4.7 At the start of a match and whenever he changes his racket during a match a player shall show his opponent and the umpire the racket he is about to use and shall allow them to examine it.

3.5 Definitions

3.5.1 A 'rally' is the period during which the ball is in play.

3.5.2 A 'let' is a rally of which the result is not scored.

3.5.3 A 'point' is a rally of which the result is scored.

3.5.4 The 'racket hand' is the hand carrying the racket.

3.5.5 The 'free hand' is the hand not carrying the racket.

3.5.6 A player 'strikes' the ball if he touches it with his racket, held in the hand, or with his racket-hand below the wrist.

3.5.7 A player 'volleys' the ball if he strikes it in play when it has not touched his court since last being struck by his opponent.

3.5.8 A player 'obstructs' the ball if he, or anything he wears or carries, touches it in play when it has not passed over the table or an imaginary extension of his end line, not having touched his court since last being struck by his opponent.

3.5.9 The 'server' is the player due to strike the ball first in the rally.

3.5.10 The 'receiver' is the player due to strike the ball second in a rally.

3.5.11 The 'umpire' is the person appointed to decide the result of each rally.

3.5.12 Anything that a player 'wears or carries' includes anything that he was wearing or carrying at the start of the rally.

3.5.13 The ball shall be regarded as passing 'over or around' the net if it passes under or outside the projection of the net assembly outside the table or if, in a return, it is struck after it has bounced back over the net.

3.6 A Good Service

3.6.1 Service shall begin with the ball resting on the palm of the free hand, which shall be stationary, open and flat, with the fingers together and the thumb free.

3.6.2 The free hand, while in contact with

the ball in service, shall at all times be above the level of the playing surface.

3.6.3   The whole of the racket shall be above the level of the playing surface from the last moment at which the ball is stationary on the palm of the free hand until the ball is struck in service.

3.6.4   The server shall then project the ball upwards, by hand only and without imparting spin, so that it rises from the palm of the hand within 45 degrees of the vertical.

3.6.5   As the ball is falling from the highest point of its trajectory the server shall strike it so that:

3.6.5.1   in singles, it touches first his court and then, passing directly over or around the net assembly, touches the receiver's court;

3.6.5.2   in doubles, it touches first his right half-court and then, passing directly over or around the net assembly, touches the receiver's half-court.

3.6.6   When the ball is struck in service, it shall be behind the end line of the server's court or any imaginary extension thereof, but not farther back than the part of the server's body, other than his arm, head or leg, which is farthest from the net.

3.6.7   It is the responsibility of the player to serve so that the umpire or assistant umpire can see that he complies with the requirements for a good service.

3.6.7.1   Except when an assistant umpire has been appointed, the umpire may, on the first occasion in a match at which he has a doubt about the correctness of a player's service, interrupt play and warn the server without awarding a point.

3.6.7.2   On any subsequent occasion in the same match at which the same player's service action is of doubtful correctness, for the same or for any other reason, the player shall not be given the benefit of the doubt and shall lose a point.

3.6.7.3   Whenever there is a clear failure by the server to comply with the requirements for a good service no warning shall be given and he shall lose a point, on the first as on any other occasion.

3.6.8   Exceptionally, strict observance of any particular requirement for a good service may be waived where the umpire is notified, before play begins, that compliance with that requirement is prevented by physical disability.

3.7   A Good Return

3.7.1   The ball, having been served and returned, shall be struck so that it passes over or around the net assembly and touches the opponent's court, either directly or after touching the net assembly.

3.8   The Order of Play

3.8.1   In singles, the server shall first make a good service, the receiver shall then make a good return and thereafter server and receiver alternately shall each make a good return.

3.8.2   In doubles, the server shall first make a good service, the receiver shall then make a good return, the partner of the server shall then make a good return, the partner of the receiver shall then make a good return and thereafter each player in turn in that sequence shall make a good return.

3.9   In Play

3.9.1   The ball shall be in play from the last moment at which it is stationary before being projected in service until

3.9.1.1   it touches anything other than the playing surface, the net assembly, the racket held in the hand or the racket hand below the wrist, or

3.9.1.2   the rally is otherwise decided as a let or a point.

3.10 A Let

3.10.1 The rally shall be a let

3.10.1.1 if in service the ball, in passing over or around the net assembly, touches it, provided the service is otherwise good or the ball is volleyed or obstructed by the receiver or his partner;

3.10.1.2 if the service is delivered when, in the opinion of the umpire, the receiving player or pair is not ready, provided that neither the receiver nor his partner attempts to strike the ball;

3.10.1.3 if, in the opinion of the umpire, failure to make a good service or a good return or otherwise to comply with the Laws is due to a disturbance outside the control of the player;

3.10.1.4 if it is interrupted to correct an error in the order of service, receiving or ends;

3.10.1.5 if it is interrupted to introduce the expedite system;

3.10.1.6 if it is interrupted to warn a player that his service is of doubtful correctness or that he has failed to notify a change of racket;

3.10.1.7 if the conditions of play are disturbed in a way which, in the opinion of the umpire, is likely to affect the outcome of the rally.

3.11 A Point

3.11.1 Unless the rally is a let, a player shall lose a point

3.11.1.1 if he fails to make a good service;

3.11.1.2 if he fails to make a good return;

3.11.1.3 if he volleys or obstructs the ball, except as provided in 3.10.1.1;

3.11.1.4 if he strikes the ball twice successively;

3.11.1.5 if the ball touches his court twice successively;

3.11.1.6 if he strikes the ball with a side of the racket blade whose surface does not comply with the requirements of 3.4.2;

3.11.1.7 if he, or anything he wears or carries, moves the playing surface while the ball is in play;

3.11.1.8 if his free hand touches the playing surface while the ball is in play;

3.11.1.9 if he, or anything he wears or carries, touches the net assembly while the ball is in play;

3.11.1.10 if, as he serves, he or his partner stamps his foot;

3.11.1.11 if, in doubles, he strikes the ball out of the sequence established by the server and receiver;

3.11.1.12 if, under the expedite system, he serves and the receiving player or pair makes thirteen successive good returns.

3.12 A Game

3.12.1 A game shall be won by the player or pair first scoring twenty-one points unless both players or pairs score twenty points, when the game shall be won by the player or pair first scoring subsequently two points more than the opposing player or pair.

3.13 A Match

3.13.1 A match shall consist of the best of three games or the best of five games.

3.13.2 Play shall be continuous throughout a match except that any player shall be entitled to claim an interval of not more than five minutes between the third and fourth games of a match and of not more than one minute between any other successive games of a match.

3.14 The Choice of Serving, Receiving and Ends

3.14.1 The right to make first choice shall be decided by lot.

3.14.2 The player or pair winning this right may:

3.14.2.1 choose to serve or receive first, when the loser shall have the choice of ends;

3.14.2.2   choose an end, when the loser shall have the choice of serving or receiving first;

3.14.2.3   require the loser to make the first choice, when the winner shall have whichever choice is not made by the loser.

3.14.3   In doubles, the pair having the right to serve first in each game shall decide which of them will do so;

3.14.3.1   in the first game of a match, the opposing pair shall then decide which of them will receive first;

3.14.3.2   in subsequent games of the match, the first receiver will be determined by the choice of server, as provided in 3.15.5.

3.15   The Order of Serving, Receiving and Ends

3.15.1   After five points have been scored the receiving player or pair shall become the serving player or pair and so on until the end of the game, or until each player or pair has scored twenty points or until the introduction of the expedite system.

3.15.2   In doubles,

3.15.2.1   the first server shall be the selected player of the pair having the right to serve first and the first receiver shall be the appropriate player of the opposing pair;

3.15.2.2   the second server shall be the player who was the first receiver and the second receiver shall be the partner of the first server;

3.15.2.3   the third server shall be the partner of the first server and the third receiver shall be the partner of the first receiver;

3.15.2.4   the fourth server shall be the partner of the first receiver and the fourth receiver shall be the first server;

3.15.2.5   the fifth server shall be the player who was the first server and the players shall thereafter serve in the same sequence until the end of the game.

3.15.3   If both players or pairs have scored twenty points or if the expedite system is in operation the sequence of serving and receiving shall be the same but each player shall serve for only one point in turn until the end of the game.

3.15.4   The player or pair who served first in a game shall receive first in the immediately subsequent game of the match.

3.15.5   In each game of a doubles match after the first, the first server having been chosen, the first receiver shall be the player who served to him in the immediately preceding game.

3.15.6   In the last possible game of a doubles match the pair due next to receive shall change the order of receiving when first either pair scores ten points.

3.15.7   The player or pair starting at one end in a game shall start at the other end in the immediately subsequent game of the match.

3.15.8   In the last possible game of a match the players shall change ends when first either player or pair scores ten points.

3.16   Out of Order of Serving, Receiving and Ends

3.16.1   If the players have not changed ends when they should have done so, play shall be interrupted by the umpire as soon as the error is discovered and shall resume with the players at the ends at which they should be at the score that has been reached, according to the sequence established at the beginning of the match.

3.16.2   If a player serves or receives out of turn, play shall be interrupted as soon as the error is discovered and shall resume with those players serving and receiving who should be server and receiver respectively at the score that has been reached, according to the sequence established at the beginning of the match and, in doubles, to the order of

3.16.3   serving chosen by the pair having the right to serve first in the game during which the error is discovered.

3.16.3   In any circumstances, all points scored before the discovery of an error shall be reckoned.

3.17   The Expedite System

3.17.1   The expedite system shall come into operation if a game is unfinished after fifteen minutes' play, or at any earlier time at the request of both players or pairs.

3.17.1.1   If the ball is in play when the time limit is reached, play shall stop and shall resume with service by the player who served in the rally that was interrupted.

3.17.1.2   If the ball is not in play when the time limit is reached, play shall resume with service by the player who received in the immediately preceding rally of the game.

3.17.2   Thereafter, each player shall serve for one point in turn, in accordance with 3.15.3, and if the rally is not decided before the receiving player or pair makes thirteen good returns the server shall lose a point.

3.17.3   Once introduced, the expedite system shall remain in operation for the remainder of the match.

REGULATIONS FOR INTERNATIONAL COMPETITIONS

4.2   Equipment and Playing Conditions

4.2.1   **Playing Equipment**

4.2.1.1   In World, Continental and Open International Championships

4.2.1.1.1   the table, the net and the ball shall each be of a brand and type

4.2.1.1.2   currently approved by the ITTF; the covering material on a side of the blade used for striking the ball shall be of a brand and type currently authorised by the ITTF;

4.2.1.1.3   the surface of one side of the racket shall be bright red and the surface of the other side shall be black, whether or not both sides are used for striking the ball.

4.2.1.2   The approval and authorisation of playing equipment shall be conducted in accordance with directives agreed by the Council.

4.2.2   **Clothing**

4.2.2.1   Playing clothing shall normally consist of a short-sleeved shirt and shorts or skirt, socks and playing shoes; other garments, such as part or all of a track suit, shall not be worn during play except with the permission of the referee.

4.2.2.2   A playing shirt, shorts or skirt shall be mainly of a uniform colour other than white, but

4.2.2.2.1   the collar and sleeves of a playing shirt may be of a contrasting colour or colours other than white;

4.2.2.2.2   the background colour may include narrow stripes, in one direction only and of a contrasting colour other than white, having a width not greater than 1mm and a spacing not less than 30mm;

4.2.2.2.3   trimming of white or any colour, contained within a total width of 10mm, may be used along the edges and side seams of a garment.

4.2.2.3   A playing garment may carry

4.2.2.3.1   the maker's normal trademark, symbol or name contained within a total area of 16 sq cm;

4.2.2.3.2   the ITTF logo, where the design has been authorised by the ITTF;

4.2.2.3.3   a badge or lettering on the front or side contained within a total area of 64 sq cm;

4.2.2.3.4   numbers or letters on the back of

4.2.2.4 a playing shirt to identify a player or his Association or, in club matches, his club.

Any markings or trimming on the front or side of a playing garment and any objects such as jewellery worn by a player shall not be so conspicuous or brightly reflecting as to unsight an opponent.

4.2.2.5 Any question of the legality or acceptability of playing clothing shall be decided by the referee, except that he may not rule illegal or unacceptable a design which has been authorised by the ITTF.

4.2.2.6 In World and Continental Championships the players of a team taking part in a team match, and players from the same Association forming a doubles pair, shall be dressed uniformly, with the possible exception of socks and shoes.

4.2.3 Playing conditions

4.2.3.1 The playing space shall not be less than 14m long, 7m wide and 4m high.

4.2.3.2 The playing area shall be enclosed by dark coloured surrounds about 75cm high, separating it from adjacent playing areas and from spectators.

4.2.3.3 The light intensity, measured at the height of the playing surface, shall not be less than 400 lux uniformly over the whole of the playing surface and the intensity at any other part of the playing area shall not be less than half the intensity over the playing surface.

4.2.3.4 The light source shall not be less than 4m above the floor.

4.2.3.5 The background shall be generally dark and shall not contain bright light sources nor daylight through uncovered windows.

4.2.3.6 The floor shall not be light-coloured nor brightly reflecting.

4.4 Match Conduct

4.4.1 **Scoring**

4.4.1.1 The umpire shall call the score immediately the ball is out of play at the completion of a rally, or as soon as is practicable thereafter taking account of any applause or other noise which may prevent the call from being heard.

4.4.1.1.1 In calling the score during a game the umpire shall call first the number of points scored by the player or pair due to serve in the next rally of the game and then the number of points scored by the opposing player or pair.

4.4.1.1.2 At the beginning of a game and before any change of server the umpire shall follow the score call by naming the next server.

4.4.1.1.3 At the end of a game the umpire shall name the winning player or pair and shall then call the number of points scored by the winning player or pair followed by the number of points scored by the losing player or pair.

4.4.1.1.4 When a rally is a let the umpire is recommended to repeat the previous score call before the next rally begins, to indicate that no point has been scored.

4.4.1.2 In addition to calling the score the umpire may use hand signals to indicate his decisions.

4.4.1.2.1 When a point has been scored, he may raise to shoulder level the hand nearer to the player or pair who won the point.

4.4.1.2.2 At the start of a game or at the change of service he may point with his hand towards the player or pair due to serve next.

4.4.1.2.3 When for any reason the rally is a let, he may raise his hand above his head to show that the rally has ended.

4.4.1.3 The server is recommended not to serve until all the players are aware of the correct score, either through hearing the umpire's score call or by seeing the score indicators; if the server frequently serves prematurely and the umpire considers that this is adversely affecting an opponent, the umpire shall warn the server to delay his service and shall, if necessary, remind the receiver to indicate, by raising his free hand, that he is not ready.

4.4.1.4 The score shall be called in the language of the Association in whose territory the competition takes place or in any other language acceptable to both players or pairs and to the umpire.

4.4.1.5 The score shall be displayed on mechanical or electrical indicators which are clearly visible to the players and, as far as is practicable, to the spectators.

4.4.1.6 When the umpire warns a player about a service of doubtful correctness he shall hold up a blue card so that it is clearly visible to the players and spectators; a player may receive only one such warning during a match, for any reason.

4.4.2 **Expedite Procedure**

4.4.2.1 The duration of play in any game in which the expedite system is not already in operation shall be monitored by the assistant umpire.

4.4.2.2 The assistant umpire shall start the clock immediately the ball is first in play in each game and shall stop and re-start it for interruptions of play other than momentary breaks; such interruptions may be due to the ball going outside the playing area, the change of ends in the last possible game of a match, towelling, adjustment of clothing, replacement of damaged equipment or recovery from a fall or injury.

4.4.2.3 At the end of fifteen minutes' play in any game in which the expedite system is not already in operation the assistant umpire shall call 'time'; play having thus been interrupted the umpire shall call 'let', shall inform the players that the remainder of the match will be played under the expedite system and

shall then re-start play, without any interval.

4.4.2.4 Thereafter, the number of each stroke made by the receiving player or pair, from one to thirteen, shall be called out so that it is clearly audible to the players.

4.4.2.4.1 The call shall be made immediately after the ball is struck.

4.4.2.4.2 The number shall be called in English or in any other language acceptable to the umpire and to both players or pairs.

4.4.2.5 If play continues after the thirteenth return the umpire shall call 'stop'.

4.4.4 **Continuity of Play**

4.4.4.1 It is the duty of the umpire to ensure that play throughout a match is continuous, except during any authorised intervals.

4.4.4.1.1 He shall allow only the shortest reasonable pauses during games for such purposes as towelling and cleaning spectacles, and wherever practicable towels and similar items shall be kept near the umpire.

4.4.4.1.2 He shall not allow these pauses to be prolonged by conversation or lingering and whenever either player or pair is ready to continue the other player or pair shall be called on to do so.

4.4.4.2 If a player breaks his racket during the play he shall replace it immediately with either another racket which he has brought with him to the playing area or one which is handed to him in the playing area.

4.4.4.3 The referee may allow a suspension of play, of the shortest practical duration, if a player is temporarily incapacitated by an accident, provided that in the opinion of the referee the suspension is not likely to be unduly disadvantageous to the opposing player or pair.

4.4.4.4 A suspension shall not be allowed for a disability which was present or was reasonably to be expected at the beginning of the match, or where it is due to the normal stress of play; disability such as cramp or exhaustion, caused by the player's current state of fitness or by the manner in which play has proceeded, does not justify such an emergency suspension, which may be allowed only for incapacity resulting from an accident, such as injury caused by a fall.

4.4.4.5 Players shall remain in or near the playing area throughout a match, except with the permission of the referee; during authorised intervals between games they shall remain within three metres of the playing area, under the supervision of the umpire.

4.4.5 **Practice**

4.4.5.1 Players are entitled to practise on the match table for up to two minutes immediately before the start of a match; the specified practice period may be extended only with the permission of the referee.

4.4.5.2 Players shall be given reasonable opportunity to check and to familiarise themselves with any equipment which they are to use, but this shall not automatically entitle them to more than a few practice rallies before resuming play after the replacement of a damaged ball or racket.

4.4.5.3 If a match cannot begin or continue because the players are unable to agree on the choice of a ball the choice shall be made at random by the umpire, and a player refusing to accept the decision may be disqualified by the referee.

4.4.5.3.1 Wherever practicable, and especially for staged events, it is recommended that players be asked to check proposed match balls before they go to the match table and to select two or three which are mutually acceptable.

4.4.5.4 Players shall not practise on the match table during the intervals between games or during any other authorised suspension of play; during an emergency suspension the referee may, at his discretion, allow players to practise on another table.

4.4.6 **Advice to Players**

4.4.6.1 A player may receive advice from anyone during the intervals between games or during any other authorised suspension of play; he shall not receive advice at any other time in a match, such as during a momentary pause for towelling or at the change of ends in the last possible game of a match.

4.4.6.2 The purpose of this restriction is to prevent distracting interruptions and to place upon the player responsibility for his own strategy and tactics during a game.

4.4.6.2.1 Association and match officials shall discourage attempts to give or to receive advice other than at the authorised times or otherwise to influence play while it is in progress.

4.4.6.2.2 If such attempts persist after a warning by the umpire he shall ask the adviser to leave the vicinity of the playing area for the remainder of the match that is in progress; if the adviser refuses to leave the umpire shall suspend play and report immediately to the referee.

4.4.6.3 This restriction applies only to advice on play and nothing in these regulations shall prevent a player or captain, as appropriate, from making a formal appeal against the decision of a match official or hinder a consultation between a player and his Association representative or interpreter on the explanation of a juridical decision.

4.4.7 **Behaviour of Players**

4.4.7.1 Umpires and captains shall discourage players from mannerisms or behaviour that may unfairly affect an opponent, may offend spectators or may bring the game into disrepute.

4.4.7.2 When the umpire considers that, for any of these reasons, the conduct of a player in the playing area is not of an acceptable standard he shall warn the player and ask him to refrain from the offending behaviour.

4.4.7.2.1 If the player persists in the conduct which was the subject of the warning the umpire shall report the matter to the referee.

4.4.7.2.2 Normally such a report shall be made at the end of the match but, if the umpire considers that the matter is sufficiently serious, he shall suspend play and report immediately to the referee.

4.4.7.3 The referee may, at his discretion, take disciplinary action against a player for persistent unfair or offensive behaviour, whether reported by the umpire or not; such action may include disqualification from an event or from a whole competition.

4.4.7.4 If a player fails to notify the umpire and his opponent when he changes his racket during a match the umpire shall immediately report the matter to the referee; on the first occasion the referee shall warn the player and on any subsequent occasion the referee shall disqualify him.

Footnote

The above rules are correct at the time of writing but are subject to alteration by the ITTF at any time.

Glossary

Anti-loop   A type of rubber that tends to lessen the effect of spin and is particularly good against loop or heavy chop.

Attack   A type of game where a player attempts to win points by forceful shots.

Backspin   The spin imparted on a ball that makes it revolve in an anticlockwise direction as it travels away from the striker.

Base Line   The white line on the edges of the ends of a table tennis table.

Block   A stroke that returns the ball with hardly any movement, using speed and spin already on the ball.

Centre Line   The line defining the area for service in doubles play.

Chop   A downward stroke that produces backspin.

Combination Bat   A bat with completely different rubbers on each side.

Controller   The player who places returns in such a manner as to allow the other player to perform set exercises or practices.

Counterhit   An attacking stroke played against a topspin, drive or loop shot.

Defence   A type of game that players can use to prevent any loss of points, whilst hoping to win points from the opponent by forced errors.

Drive   A forceful shot relying more on speed, with only an element of spin.

Drop Shot   A stroke that is played close to the net with deadening effect to deceive an opponent.

Feeder   The player who places balls to a pupil whilst he is undergoing practice.

Flick   A stroke using the wrist as the main driving force.

Float   A stroke that produces little or no spin, but appears to have a similar action to a chop or backspin.

Half-volley   A ball that is taken very early just after it has bounced.

Hammer Grip   This grip is similar to one holding a hammer with no fingers running up the blade of bat.

High Defence   Sometimes described as a lob. The ball is played back with considerable height and is more effective when given a large degree of spin. It is often used by players experiencing trouble who wish to give themselves more time.

Inverted Rubber   Rubber that is stuck onto a bat with the pimples facing inwards.

Kill   A stroke that is designed to win the point using maximum power.

Loop   A stroke that produces a very heavy

117

Glossary

topspin so that the ball travels in a loop before bouncing on opponent's court. There are many versions from slow loops, fast loops and loop drives. All are designed to confuse the opponent with spin and/or speed variations of an intense level.

Pen Grip   The grip most favoured by Asian players, who hold the handle between thumb and forefinger in a similar manner to a pen. There are slight variations between the Chinese and Japanese with regard to the placing of the other fingers against the back of bat. Not generally considered to be as effective as the orthodox grip for Western players, because of the incredible agility needed to cope with the backhand side of the table.

Push   A basic stroke used for control and placement.

Ready Position   The position players take up when ready to commence a point. A good position would generally be considered to be an arm's length from the table edge.

Roll   A term recently used for a stroke that uses the wrist to turn the ball back to the opponent.

Sandwich Bat   A bat that uses sponge and rubber rather than just rubber as the playing surface.

Sidespin   The spin imparted on a ball that makes it revolve horizontally whilst travelling towards the opponent.

Smash   A power stroke with the emphasis on speed, with the intention of winning the point. Also called a flat hit or kill.

Topspin   The spin imparted on a ball to make it revolve in a clockwise direction as it travels away from the striker.

Unforced Error   A lost point due more to the lack of judgement or skill of the player rather than the skill of the opponent.

Useful Addresses

The International Table Tennis Federation
53 London Road
St Leonards on Sea
Sussex TN37 6AY
England

European Table Tennis Union
43 Knowsley Road
Smithills
Bolton
Lancashire BL1 6JH

English Table Tennis Association
21 Claremont
Hastings
Sussex TN34 1HA

New Zealand Table Tennis Association
PO Box 867
Wellington
New Zealand

Table Tennis Association of Wales
198 Cynoed Road
Cardiff CF2 6BQ

Scottish Table Tennis Association
18 Ainslie Place
Edinburgh EH3 6AU

Irish Table Tennis Association
4 Fairhill Gardens
Belfast BT15 4FZ

English Schools Association
Engelberg
Badger Lane
Woolly Moor
Derbyshire DE56 F3G

Association of Table Tennis Players
25 Brookside Crescent
Cuffley
Hertfordshire

Index

Crowood Sports Books

Badminton – The Skills of the Game	Peter Roper
Basketball – The Skills of the Game	Paul Stimpson
Canoeing – Skills and Techniques	Neil Shave
*The Skills of Cricket	Keith Andrew
Fitness for Sport	Rex Hazeldine
*Golf – The Skills of the Game	John Stirling
Hockey – The Skills of the Game	John Cadman
Judo – Skills and Techniques	Tony Reay
Jumping	Malcolm Arnold
Rugby Union – The Skills of the Game	Barrie Corless
Skiing – Developing Your Skill	John Shedden
Sprinting and Hurdling	Peter Warden
Squash – The Skills of the Game	Ian McKenzie
Swimming	John Verrier
Table Tennis – The Skills of the Game	Gordon Steggall
Volleyball – The Skills of the Game	Keith Nicholls

* Also available in paperback

Further details of titles available or in preparation can be obtained from the publishers.